# THE VISIONS OF SAINT
# FRANCES OF ROME

# THE VISIONS OF SAINT FRANCES OF ROME

## HELL, PURGATORY, AND HEAVEN REVEALED

by
Saint Frances of Rome

Translated and edited by
Fr. Robert Nixon, OSB

TAN Books
Gastonia, North Carolina

Translated by Fr. Robert Nixon, OSB

Cover design by Andrew Schmalen

Cover image: *Last Judgment* by Giovanni De Min. 1824. Fresco. Mondadori Portfolio / Electa / Luigi Baldin / Bridgeman Images.

ISBN: 978-1-5051-3155-0
Kindle ISBN: 978-1-5051-3156-7
ePUB ISBN: 978-1-5051-3157-4

Published in the United States by
TAN Books
PO Box 269
Gastonia, NC 28053
www.TANBooks.com

Printed in the United States of America

*I am Alpha and Omega; the beginning and the end.*
*To him that thirsteth, I will give freely of the fountain of*
*the water of life.*
*(. . .)*
*But the fearful, and unbelieving, and the abominable,*
*and murderers, and whoremongers, and sorcerers,*
*and idolaters, and all liars,*
*they shall have their portion in the pool burning with*
*fire and brimstone,*
*which is the second death.*

Revelation 21:6, 8

# Contents

## Selected Other Visions of Saint Frances of Rome

# Translator's Introduction

It is fitting that heaven, purgatory, and hell should be matters not only of perennial interest but of the greatest and most intense concern to all Christians. For these three states represent the various possible destinations of our immortal soul—heaven and hell as eternal realities, with purgatory as a temporally limited place of purification and penance. If we concern ourselves (as most of us necessarily do) with the things of this present world, which are merely passing and contingent, how much more should our hearts be occupied with those realms of existence which endure forever and ever? If we give serious attention to what happens to us during our earthly life, which lasts just a few short years, how much more should we strive for happiness and peace in that future life which shall have no end?

Throughout the generations, there have been innumerable attempts to depict or imagine the spiritual realities of heaven, purgatory, and hell, both in the visual and musical arts, and in literature. More importantly, numerous saints have received visions and revelations pertaining to the nature of hell, purgatory, and heaven. Among these revelations, the visions of Saint Frances of Rome (1384–1440) must be given an honored and distinguished place. Frances was a holy Roman woman of illustrious, wealthy, and noble lineage, who was granted the grace of visions in a particularly vivid and powerful way. Moreover, she had a wonderful spiritual director and confessor, Canon Giovanni Matteotti, to whom she would describe these visions in precise and dramatic detail. Matteotti, in turn, took the greatest care to commit these illuminating and inspiring revelations to writing; both as a witness to the sanctity of Frances and for the spiritual benefit and edification of future readers.

Astonishingly, the most epic and complex series of visions experienced by St. Frances—encompassing, hell, purgatory, and heaven—all took place on a single day.[1] During this time, the saint was afflicted by a very grave illness and, in turn, was confined to her bedchamber.

---

[1] The editors of the *Acta Sanctorum* opine that this must have occurred sometime after 1432. As Saint Frances died in the year 1440, this means that the visions were experienced towards the end of her life.

There, the eyes of her soul were opened to obtain an unforgettable glimpse into these most awesome and stupendous mysteries. On the evening of that same momentous day, she confided all that she had witnessed and experienced to her trusted spiritual director, making these revelations under holy obedience[2] to that faithful priest. The diligent Canon Matteotti then meticulously made a written record of everything which she had said. The result is a remarkable and unique work of visionary literature, which is here presented for the first time in English.

The visions which St. Frances revealed are detailed, complex, and often intensely harrowing. In particular, the torments of hell, which comprise by far the largest portion of the work, are described in often gruesome and horrifying detail.[3] Nevertheless, as she witnessed

---

[2]  The narrations which follow often mention that Saint Frances shared her revelations *under holy obedience,* after having been asked to do so by her spiritual director. This holy obedience reflects the obedience of St. Frances to the Church, in the person of its minister (i.e., the priest who was appointed as her confessor and spiritual director.) It also reflects her fidelity to the Benedictine charism of obedience to religious superiors.

[3]  The reason for the shortness of the section on heaven (compared to those on hell and purgatory) is explained by Saint Frances's own observation that "there were many things in her visions of heaven which she could not comprehend, and that those things

all these things, St. Frances relates that she was accompanied by the archangel Raphael as her unfailing companion and guide. This powerful angel imbued her with courage and strength, both by his reassuring presence and his inspiring words of exhortation.

The modern reader will inevitably be struck by certain resemblances to Dante's poetic masterpiece, *The Divine Comedy*, which was completed about a century before St. Frances had her visions. However, Dante's immortal poem was a work of pure artistic inspiration, imagination, and literary genius, whereas the writings of St. Frances were a genuine and inspired revelation, given by the grace of God in response to her intense prayer and contemplation.

These writings fall within the category of work that is described as *private revelations*. Private revelations of this type, though genuinely and authentically experienced by the person concerned, do not make any claims to doctrinal authority. They are necessarily filtered through the cultural, historical, and personal perspective of the person receiving them; this biased perspective will generally tend to contribute something to the private revelations' color, content, and form. Therefore, there are several

---

which she did witness, she perceived only in an unclear and obscure way."

passages in these visions (such as St. Frances's description of limbo) which should not be read as authoritative statements of Catholic doctrine. All passages of this type are identified in footnotes. Saint Frances herself, at the end of the work, very prudently states that she wishes everything she has related be subjected to the judgment and magisterium of the Holy Catholic Church. The modern reader should, of course, bear this humble reservation in mind at all times. Saint Frances was not a dogmatic theologian, but a mystic and a visionary. She was not concerned with explicating or expounding questions of doctrine and dogma, but rather of her own direct spiritual experience and insights afforded to her by the grace of God.

To this wonderful saint's momentous and unforgettable visions of hell, purgatory, and heaven, have been added a small selection of other visions that St. Frances received from the years 1430–1434. These were similarly narrated to and carefully recorded by Canon Giovanni Matteotti. If the visions of hell and purgatory (which constitute by far the largest part of this volume) are generally utterly terrifying and heart-rending, most of these other selected visions are suffused with a radiant and enchanting beauty. Thus, they form a perfect and fitting counterpart to the major work offered here.

As has been noted, St. Frances of Rome was an Italian noblewoman of extraordinary piety and sanctity. Despite feeling a vocation to consecrated religious life during her childhood, she was married at a young age, and so became a wife and mother—fulfilling both roles with the most admirable and exemplary love and devotion. After some years, with the consent and understanding of her devout and religious husband, she established a convent for women, following the Rule of Saint Benedict. These pious women were Benedictine *oblates* rather than nuns; meaning that they lived an enclosed, religious life without being bound by any formal or public vows. By the grace of God, the convent founded by St. Frances has continued to exist and operate into our own times. In Latin, it is known by the beautiful and evocative name of the *Turris Speculorum,* or in Italian the *Tor de'Specchi* (meaning "The Tower of Mirrors").

Today, St. Frances of Rome is venerated as the patroness saint of Benedictine oblates, widows, and (very curiously) automobile drivers.[4] A translation of the life of

---

[4] Saint Frances was declared patroness of automobile drivers in 1925 by Pope Pius XI, on account of a popular tradition that whenever St. Frances traveled the streets of Rome, an angel would go before her with a lantern to light her way. Reference to this miraculous

the saint found in the Tridentine *Breviarium Romanum* is included immediately after this introduction.

The source of the texts for the visions of Saint Frances is the *Acta Sanctorum,* March, Volume II, published in Antwerp in 1668, which compiles Matteotti's written records. The literary style of the original is vivid, dramatic, and colorful, but sometimes exhibits a certain confusion of structure and repetitiveness. The original text also features a considerable number of expressions of ambiguous meaning (apparently derived from colloquial, late-Medieval Italian words now fallen into disuse), which even the learned editors of the *Acta Sanctorum* have not always been able to determine with complete certainty. In preparing this edition, the translator has endeavored to render the meaning faithfully into idiomatic and comprehensible English. In some cases, a certain amount of informed conjecture, paraphrase, and literary license has been employed to do this. We leave it to the reader to judge the success, or otherwise, of this humble attempt.

It is hoped that these powerful and often startling visions may awaken the soul of each reader not only to genuine fear and horror of the eternal punishments of

phenomenon appears in one of the visions contained here. See the chapter entitled, "The visions of Saint Frances commence."

hell, but also (and more importantly) to a passionate yearning for the unimaginable glories of heaven. For it is to that place of everlasting and transcendent happiness and ineffable splendor that God wishes to lead us all, through the merits and mercy of His Only Begotten Son, Our Lord Jesus Christ, who lives and reigns forever and ever. Amen.

Fr. Robert Nixon, OSB,
Translator and editor,
*Abbey of the Most Holy Trinity,*
*New Norcia, Western Australia*

# The Life of Saint Frances of Rome from the *Breviarium Romanum ex Decreto SS. Concilii Tridentini Restitutum*

Frances, a noblewoman of Rome, gave illustrious signs of her virtue from a tender age. Even as a young girl, she disdained the trivialities and flippancies of childish games and all the vanities and temptations of the world, delighting instead in the refuge of solitude and deep prayer.

At the age of eleven, she earnestly consecrated her virginity to the Lord, and resolved to enter a convent as a nun. Nevertheless, her parents could not be persuaded to grant her permission to do so, despite all her efforts. Rather, in humble obedience to these parents [when she had reached the age of marriage], Frances was wedded to a certain young man of distinguished affluence and nobility, called Lorenzo Ponziano.[5]

After her marriage, she continued to cultivate a life of strict prayer and penance as much as her status and responsibilities as a wife permitted her to do so. Except when compelled by some unavoidable obligation, she studiously avoided theaters, banquets, parties, and other worldly and secular entertainments. Contrary to the custom of most women of her wealth and position, she always wore very simple attire of common wool. Whatever spare time she had from her domestic duties, she diligently devoted herself to prayer and the performance of charitable works for her neighbors and the poor. A particular concern of hers was to help guide other married noblewomen to cultivate their spiritual lives, and to avoid the sins and vanities which were then so prevalent among persons of that class.

For this purpose, she established a house of Benedictine oblates in the city of Rome. In this religious house, or convent, women were able to live a life of prayer and enclosure in the manner of consecrated nuns, but without binding themselves by any formal vows. Frances did this while her husband, Lorenzo, was still alive, for

---

[5]    In the circles and times in which Saint Frances lived, arranged marriages for young women were very much the norm.

he graciously granted her his permission and blessing to consecrate her life more fully to God in this manner.

But misfortunate was soon to befall this holy woman. First, her husband was sent into exile, and then the family was deprived of all its wealth and social standing. However, Frances remained perfectly steadfast and committed herself to her religious life with even greater stricture and austerity. She considered herself to be a mother of all those who needed her assistance, including the poorest and most degraded and wretched of the women and girls of Rome. She kept long vigils of prayer and subsisted each day on a single meal of herbs, legumes, and pure water.

Frances was graced with innumerable visions and spiritual graces. Often when witnessing the elevation of the Most Blessed Sacrament, she would be taken up into an ecstasy of celestial contemplation and would remain physically immobile for some time. She was often severely vexed by many demons, but was granted a very powerful guardian angel, whose presence she is reported to have been able to see clearly.

Distinguished by many astonishing miracles and pious virtues, Frances departed from this world to enter the glories of heaven in the fifty-sixth year of her life. Her name was added to the canon of saints by Pope Paul V.[6]

---

[6]  Saint Frances was canonized by Pope Paul V in 1608.

# THE VISIONS OF HELL, PURGATORY, AND HEAVEN OF SAINT FRANCES OF ROME

*as recorded by her spiritual director,*
Canon Giovanni Matteotti

# Saint Frances commences her narration to her spiritual father

Once it happened that Blessed Frances was gravely afflicted by illness and so confined to her bedchamber. While there, not wishing the time to be wasted, she devoted herself wholeheartedly to the most intense prayer and contemplation. As evening fell and the hour for vespers approached, her spiritual father entered her room to visit her and inquire about the state of her health. At once, he perceived from the expression on her countenance that she had undergone some very deep mystical experience that day, and he asked her (under the bonds of religious obedience) to relate to him all that had taken place. Frances replied that, after much prayer and contemplation, she had been taken up into a spiritual ecstasy. The will of God had then led her soul forth from her body to inspect the realms of hell, purgatory, and heaven.

Under holy obedience, she began first to describe her visions of hell. As she entered those infernal regions, she saw there a vast and unfathomable abyss of unspeakable horror and unimaginable foulness. Even to speak or think of this place was, she testified, a source of the most grave trembling and fear for her. Nevertheless, as one committed to the charism of obedience, she was prepared to follow the directions of her spiritual director and tell him all her experiences honestly and without reservation. So, in a state of holy fear and reverence, she proceeded to relate all that she had witnessed, in accordance with the commands of Holy Mother Church, as expressed through her appointed spiritual father.

What she related to him is recorded accurately in the following pages.

# The geography of hell
# and the state of limbo

At the entrance of hell, there was an enormous and imposing inscription written in grim and dreadful lettering of dark crimson—the color, indeed, of congealed blood. This ominous inscription ran thus:

"BEHOLD, THIS PLACE IS HELL,
WHERE SOULS CONDEMNED MUST DWELL.
OF ALL THE LANDS ACCURSED
THIS IS BY FAR THE WORST!
FROM PAIN THERE IS NO REST
WITHIN THESE REALMS UNBLESSED:
THE FLAMES HERE BURN FOREVER,
THE TORMENT CEASES NEVER!"

In this dreaded region, Blessed Frances was to see, hear, and sense many things of infinite and indescribable terror. It was, as she recalls, as if she was taken out of herself, and suffused with such an intense and all-consuming fear and horror that it could scarcely be imagined or put into words.

But at the same time, she felt a certain powerful and benign presence beside her, which she could not, however, perceive with her physical senses. Nevertheless, this mysterious and kindly presence seemed to urge her to take courage and not to let dread overcome her.

Now, the entrance to this infernal place had been (as has been mentioned) unimaginably dreadful and imposing. But within, it was even worse—much, much worse! For there were dense clouds and opaque shadows of an almost palpable darkness, which no human words could ever suffice to express, nor human senses could comprehend. This realm, hell, was divided into three parts: an uppermost part; a middle part, of greater and more severe torments than the first; and finally, a nethermost region, where the punishments and sufferings reached infinite and unbounded extremity. Between each of these parts, or levels, vast and empty regions of space were interposed, which were filled with hideous black nebulae and swirling, lightless mists.

Of all the creatures and entities which inhabited this infernal kingdom, there was one who stood out as the largest and most dominant of them all—an enormous and ancient dragon. Indeed, this beast was present in all three of the levels of hell, with his head in the uppermost level, his body in the middle level, and his tail reaching into the nethermost region. His gigantic and monstrous head, posited in the top level, was turned towards the entrance. And his hideous mouth gaped open, with his tongue hanging out in a sinister fashion. Out of this opened orifice poured a fire that burned with scorching intensity, yet it emitted no light. A putrescent and nauseating stench also issued from his mouth. Similarly, black fire—hot, fetid, and lightless—also seeped through his eyes and ears.

There, Frances, the handmaid of God, heard also great wailings and cries. These ululations[7] filled the ear, articulating horrid and appalling blasphemies, together with the most wretched laments of dolor[8] and distress. And as Frances attempted to describe to her spiritual father the torments and lamentations which she had perceived, she herself was filled with an unspeakable pain and sorrow, and she began to break down in tears.

Indeed, she narrated that as she witnessed this multitude of horrors, she felt completely overwhelmed and

---

[7]    Lamentations or wailings.

[8]    Pain.

as if she were about to faint away. But then she recalled that, at that point, the unseen, benign presence, who had exhorted her to courage earlier, again comforted her. Later on, it was revealed to her that this spiritual presence was, in fact, none other than the mighty archangel Raphael himself.

Frances saw there also the prince of the fallen angels, Satan (or Lucifer). His countenance was utterly terrifying, and he sat positioned upon a wooden beam in the middle region of the inferno. His head reached into the uppermost region, while his feet reached to the bottom level. Thus he lay, effectively occupying all three parts of hell simultaneously. His arms and legs were extended outwards, yet in such a way that they bore no likeness to a cross (for that holy form is strictly not permitted in hell). He was crowned with a kind of sinister tiara, resembling the antlers of some great deer or elk. And out of the main horns of these antlers, innumerable smaller horns sprang forth, with sparks and flames issuing from each. Metallic chains, glowing red hot, were bound around his hands, feet, and torso. One of these chains extended from Satan to the great dragon that Frances had seen before.

Frances, the handmaid of the Lord, also saw innumerable other, lesser demons. These were passing freely in and out from hell to the world, and from the world back to hell. To the accompaniment of dreadful clamors and outcries, they dragged with them the condemned souls of those whom they had managed to ensnare or deceive. The demons mocked and derided these lost souls mercilessly, with such appalling utterances that they cannot be repeated here nor committed to writing. And Frances herself sensed the pain and despair which filled these unfortunate victims with such a degree of intensity that, even as she tried to describe it to her spiritual director, she again broke down utterly in tears of piteous melancholy.

These demons, grasping the souls which they had claimed for hell, led them through the grim entrance of the unhallowed inferno. They hurled some into the flaming mouth of the great dragon, which gaped open nearby. These souls were swallowed by the dragon, but then after a while foully regurgitated, covered in disgusting and acrid mucous. At this point, they were led before a certain magistrate or high officer of the demons. Before this fiery, infernal magistrate, the case of each particular soul was carefully considered. Then the most appropriate region of hell and form of torments were determined for it on the basis of the sins and crimes it had committed and the vices to which it had succumbed during its earthly life. They were then forcibly taken to their destined place of punishment, to the cacophonous and clamorous accompaniment of indescribable weepings and wailings.

Frances then related that the journey of these souls to their destined places was by no means quick or immediate, as it was (as she later saw) for the souls who were released from purgatory and carried off to enjoy the glories of heaven. For both heaven and hell consist of three distinct levels. In the case of the supernal[9] realm of eternal glory and splendor, the three levels are, in ascending order: the heaven of the stars, the heaven of crystal, and the Empyrean heaven.[10] Both the three levels of heaven and the three levels of hell are separated from each other by incalculable distances. But, to return specifically to hell, on account of the dense, obsidian darkness and impenetrable, opaque fogs which pervade it, all motion and movement there were rendered indescribably slow, laborious, and oppressively painful.

---

9   Celestial.

10   The Empyrean heaven was a name given to the highest and most transcendent level of the heavens. This description of the geography of heaven is very similar to that presented in Dante's *Divine Comedy*. It reflects the influence of the cosmology of Aristotle, whose scientific and philosophical works were given great authority at the time.

The saint saw that some of the souls led through the gates of hell by various demons were not cast into the mouth of the dragon. Rather, they were led directly to the aforementioned magistrate of the demons and stood before him unchained. But they were then similarly judged, and then handed over to the appropriate demons to undergo their due torments. These were the souls who were guilty of less serious crimes and were therefore to remain on the uppermost level of the inferno. Even there, though, their torments were endless and unspeakable. This upper region was populated by numberless demons, some in the form of vipers, some in the form of toads, some in the form of other horrid and nameless beasts. Here were tormented the souls of Christians who were negligent of their faith, or who failed to make proper confession before passing away. Frances was appalled and shocked to witness this, but her invisible companion (who was, as has been noted, the archangel Raphael) again urged her to be strong and take courage.

At this point, Frances perceived another being or entity—an angel, not a devil—who stood near the gates of hell. The place where he was located was a little beyond the reach of the great dragon, and beyond the grasp of Lucifer, enchained (as he was) to his wooden beam. Nor was it touched at all by the noxious flames which emerged from the inferno. This place is called *limbo.* It was here that the holy patriarchs and prophets, who lived before the time of Christ, had waited patiently and hopefully for so long for the day when the Savior would come to release them from their bondage.[11] This place, limbo, is free from fire and freezing cold, and from the serpents, demons, and foul stenches of hell. Here, there is no weeping, nor wailing, nor blasphemy, nor any torments at all; but rather a calm, motionless, and peaceful condition of somnolent shadow and dreamless slumber. This is the place were infants who have not been baptized find their rest. In limbo, as in heaven and hell, there are three levels that are of different degrees of darkness. The highest level, where the shadow is lightest, is where infants conceived by good Christian parents, but who pass away before they are baptized, rest in painless peace. The second level, which is somewhat darker, is where the unbaptized, but innocent, offspring of non-Christians dwell,

---

[11]  Reference to this descent of Christ to the underworld (here interpreted as limbo) is to be found in the Apostles' Creed: ". . . *descendit ad infernos.*" The literal and original meaning of infernos in Latin is simply "lower regions." The contemporary meaning of *inferno* as a place of fire is an etymological extrapolation of its original sense.

who pass away in their infancy.[12] The third and darkest region of limbo is where infants conceived by monks or nuns or priests, or from incestuous relationships, and who die without receiving the sacrament of baptism, are bound to remain.[13]

---

[12] The original text here reads: *"parvuli concepti ex Hebraeis, et in infantile aetate mortui."* It seems likely that Frances intended this to include the unbaptized infants of all non-Christian peoples, which is reflected in the present translation.

[13] This description of the fate of unbaptized and illegitimate infants should not be read as an official Church teaching. It does, however, reflect the view which was prevalent and generally accepted at the time.

# The punishments for perverts, usurers, and blasphemers

Following this vision of the grim and foreboding portals of hell and of the shadow-realm of limbo, Frances, the holy handmaid of the Lord, was then led to the lower regions of the inferno, where multifarious and gruesome torments were carried out as the apt punishments for various particular sins of the most grave and grievous variety. Needless to say, her gentle soul was utterly stupefied and terrified by all that she witnessed there.

Firstly, she was taken to the place where those who were guilty of what are customarily described as sins against nature[14] received their eternal chastisement. This place of torment was located in one of the nethermost and darkest pits of hell, and it served as the

---

[14] Here, the Latin text reads: *"miseros homines et faeminas in sodomitico peccato implicatos, et in quolibet alio peccato contra naturam . . ."*

26

everlasting home of those depraved souls who had indulged in sexual lusts and perversities contrary to the good and wholesome ordering of divine and natural law. Here were crowds of demons, each bearing in their claw-like hands heated rods resembling iron javelins, which glowed with red-hot intensity. Upon one of these instruments of torment, the soul of each depraved malefactor and pervert was impaled, the spear entering through the posterior orifice. This fiery spear was then drawn out through the mouth of the condemned wretch, passing through their entire body—either quickly and violently, or with excruciating and protracted slowness. And from this hideous and ever-repeated process, there was neither rest nor respite.

But this was not the only form of punishment taking place. For as varied and bizarre are the acts of human perversity, lust, and sexual abuse, so correspondingly varied were the tortures which were inflicted upon those guilty of them. In truth, both these crimes and their punishments can scarcely be decently repeated or recorded in writing but are best left to the imagination of any who dare to imagine them. The whole area was filled with fetid foulness, rank, unspeakable miasmas,[15]

---

[15]  A noxious or poisonous atmosphere.

and scorching fires and chilling winds. The air echoed with blasphemous and agonized exclamations, which were reiterated without end.

Frances, whose soul was pure and whose heart was innocent, was almost overcome with shock and horror at what she witnessed there. But her celestial companion and protector, the archangel Raphael, held her trembling hand with comforting strength and urged her to take courage.

Next, Frances saw the place, located in one of the lowest regions of hell, where corrupt money lenders and those guilty of the crime of usury are tormented. Their bodies were laid upon a burning, fiery counting-table, and their limbs forcibly stretched out. However, though their limbs were extended, they did not assume the form of a cross, for—as Raphael explained to her—that holy sign or form was not permitted anywhere in hell. Demons stood all around them with vessels filled with molten gold and silver. They poured this gleaming and scalding liquid down the throats of each of the tormented souls. And with sharp implements, they carved a kind of deep incision and pit in the flesh of each one, in close proximity to the hearts of their victims, and similarly poured the molten precious metals into this bleeding opening. As they did so, the demons declared with cruel mockery and bitter derision: "O wretched, avaricious souls! Remember how desperately you longed for gold and silver while you lived. Recall how closely you always held these gleaming metals to your insatiable and miserly hearts. Well, now you may have your fill of it, and more!"

The servant of God, Frances, was utterly astonished at this most grisly and gruesome sight. She was also somewhat perplexed at how apparently physical objects and tools, such as knives and metal vessels, were able to exist and be used in hell. But her companion angel, Raphael, explained that these things appeared in her vision to be such, but they were not, in reality, physical things at all. Rather, they represented, through the medium of physical images, the spiritual torments which the souls there experienced.

The souls of those guilty of the crimes of usury and financial exploitation were, after a time, removed from the burning counting-table on which they had been stretched and tormented. They were then immersed in glass vessels which were similarly filled with molten gold or silver. They would remain in one vessel for a certain period of time, suffering unspeakable scorching and pains all the while, and then be removed and placed into another. In this way, no form of rest or respite was ever possible for them, for they could not grow accustomed to any one location or condition. And they, like all the other tormented souls, continually cried forth in a litany of mournful, lugubrious[16] lamentations and hideous and heinous blasphemies.

Frances then looked around and noticed the continual procession of souls entering hell and being led to their fitting places of suffering. She noticed that each one had upon his or her forehead a sheet of paper or card upon which the catalogue of the sins of which he or she had been convicted was inscribed. Thus, she was able to read clearly and exactly what each one was guilty of—and not only this, but by some form of revelation, she could perceive into the very depths of their being, to see and fully comprehend all the misdeeds and atrocities which weighed on their consciences. But this grace was granted to her alone, for these cards placed upon the foreheads of the damned were not visible to any other condemned souls.

She noticed also that every condemned soul had two demons assigned to it. One of these demons was employed in carrying out the actual punishments, such as those described in the course of this narration. But

---

[16] Dismal or gloomy.

the task of the other one was to remind the wretched sufferers of their sins and crimes, and also of all the good deeds they had neglected to do. In this way, each condemned soul suffered in a double sense—both from the torments afflicted upon it, and a continually renewed sense of guilt and shame. This oppressive and unrelenting sense of guilt and shame was accompanied by a poignant and painful regret at the loss of the joys of heaven, which so easily could have been attained by a few timely works of piety and penance performed while mortal life had endured.

Next, Frances was transported to the dreadful and darksome abode where those stubborn and miserable souls who had blasphemed against God and His holy saints were compelled to dwell and there to suffer ceaseless scourges and sorrows as a just retribution. Here, there were demons who bore ghastly pincers in their nefarious and agile hands. With these grim instruments of satanic surgery, they would deftly extract the tongue of each blasphemer and cast it—still writhing like some hideous, headless worm—upon a pit of burning coals which was nearby. Then, with the same pincers, the demons would take some of these coals and stuff them into the bleeding, tongueless mouth of the blasphemer. Next, they would seize the entire body of their victim and immerse it in a vat of heated oil, smoking and boiling with fiendish ebullition. Then, taking up a vessel of this same super-heated oil, they would mercilessly pour it down the throat of the blasphemer. The demonic torturers would add mockery and scorn to these torments, saying: "O miserable and deluded Soul, how could you dare to blaspheme the holy name of your Creator? With your mouth you insulted Him, and now that same despicable mouth is filled with pain. Yes, now you pay the price for your blasphemy, and you shall keep on paying it, over and over again, forever and ever, for eons without number!"

In close proximity to the impious and arrogant souls of the blasphemers were all those who had denied the Catholic Faith while they lived, because of cowardly fear of punishment or persecution, or for desire for some worldly advancement. These did not suffer quite so grievously as those guilty of deliberate and willful blasphemy, yet they were still tormented endlessly with fierce fire and burning brimstone.

Frances was almost overcome by these bitter visions, and she trembled with fear and horror. Yet her angelic guide and companion, Raphael, once more clasped her hand reassuringly. "Fear not, beloved Frances," he said in a voice both powerful and compassionate, "for what you see is but fitting justice. Never shall such scourges touch you, for *you* are certainly not destined for this place, but for God's golden realms of infinite glory!" Upon hearing this, the saint immediately took heart, and accompanied by her guardian angel, she bravely continued her journey through hell.

# The punishments for traitors, murderers, apostates, and schismatics

The next place of torment which was revealed to Saint Frances was the chamber of horrors where the contemptible souls of traitors received the just retribution for their perfidy and treachery. Here were ruthless demons, each equipped with gleaming steel forceps. They would force these instruments down the throat of each traitor and deep into their innards. There, firmly seizing each traitorous heart, they would draw the beating organ up through the throat, until it filled the whole mouth. Then, with a violent jerk, they would extract it completely, dragging the whole esophagus (now turned inside out) along with it! Once this ghoulish procedure was completed, the victim would then be made to swallow his heart again, so that the punishment could be repeated. But this repetition was not made any more bearable by its familiarity. Rather, because of the sheer agony of this repulsive act, each time it was repeated, it was anticipated by its victim with ever greater shudders of terror and trepidation.

Frances was naturally aghast at this chilling spectacle; but she, being of an inquisitive and penetrating intellect, was also somewhat perplexed by it. For she wondered how an apparently physical heart could possibly be extracted from these beings, since they were now souls without corporeal bodies. The angel Raphael sensed her question and perplexity, and he responded promptly: "Although these souls now lack the mortal flesh which they possessed while on the earth, when anyone arrives to this place of endless torment, he is punished physically, according to the parts of his body which he used to commit his sins. Thus, these souls are clothed with a kind of material substance with which to feel pain after their Particular Judgement; although this material substance is not their own true, natural body. But of course, when the Final Judgement arrives, every soul will be united with its own natural body—which will then be afflicted, together with the soul, for all eternity, with chastisements similar to those which you now witness."[17]

---

[17] Following *Particular* Judgement (which occurs immediately after death), souls are separated from their own body. But at

Returning her attention to the plight of the souls of traitors, Frances saw that, after the grisly procedure of the extraction of their hearts had been repeated many times, they were next seized and hurled into a huge cauldron, which was unspeakably grimy, sooty, and filled with boiling tar. A horde of malevolent fiends stood around this cauldron. These demons would violently grasp the heads of any of the condemned which rose from the mixture, as they struggled to free themselves from the suffocating agony of the boiling, pitch-black fluid. Then they would submerge them once more, headfirst, into the putrid and acrid substance. Meanwhile, they poured out a flood of invective upon them, exclaiming: "O lying and deceitful traitors! Your minds were filled with treachery and duplicity while you lived. How perfidiously[18] did you betray your earthly lords, and also your heavenly Lord! For you were each baptized into the Truth, and therefore you renounced Satan, who is our own master here. And yet, for the sake of the empty promises and pomps of

---

the Final Judgement (which occurs at the end of time) the souls and bodies of both the blessed and condemned will be eternally reunited. The question Frances raises is how apparently physical punishments can be imposed on the non-corporeal souls of those who have not yet been reunited to their resurrected bodies.

[18] Faithless or treacherous.

the mendacious[19] monarch of hell, you betrayed the divine Truth itself and discarded your own God-given integrity!

> Your lives were one great lie.
> So, hope for you must die!
> Deceitful to the core,
> You'll burn here evermore!"

Anxiety and anguish swept down upon Frances like great black clouds—both on account of these macabre visions and the menacing proximity of the great fire-breathing dragon (mentioned earlier), whose immense head, body, and tail occupied the whole of hell. But the archangel Raphael exhorted her to take comfort, assuring her that he was beside her constantly to protect her from any harm and to shield her from all evil. Once Frances had been thus encouraged and fortified by him, they proceeded next to that dark region where the souls of murderers received their retribution.

Blood abounded in this most gory abode, which was specially furnished as an apt dwelling place for those whose souls and hands were stained with innocent blood. For here there were great vats filled with this

---

[19] Untruthful or dishonest.

vermillion fluid, heated until it boiled furiously, and gave off a stomach-turning stench of sanguine slaughter. There were also cauldrons filled with chunks of jagged ice, gleaming coldly like cruel crystal. And the demonic thralls who served in this infernal region would thrust the wicked soul of each murderer into one vessel (either one filled with boiling blood or one filled with ice). Then, after a time, it would suddenly remove it and place it in the other. This violent and revolting alternation between the extremities of heat and cold made the experience all the more horrifying and sickening for those who endured it.

But this was not the only form of torment there. For there were other demons equipped with clubs, which were ablaze with acrid fire. They used these weapons to inflict additional pain upon the souls of various murderers, while they were not being immersed in the blood and ice, as described above. Sharp, scalding blows were directed at their hearts and tongues, leaving smoking burn marks and crimson welts.

Frances noted (with some surprise) that among the souls of the murderers, there were a large number of young women present, many of whom were apparently respectable personages of high status. She recognized these as mothers who, by means of wicked arts, had deliberately brought about the death or miscarriage of unborn infants within their own wombs in order to hide the shame of illicit pregnancy or to avoid the inconvenience of having an unwanted child. These were punished in a similar manner to the other murderers, as narrated above—but also with particular modes of torment (which cannot be decently described here) that were suited to the horrendous nature of their crimes. Let it suffice to say that these corresponded to the various techniques and methods they had used to commit infanticide.

The saint also saw the place of punishment for the souls of those guilty of apostasy (or the denial of the truths of the Catholic faith) and schismatics (or those who had brought about division in the Holy Church). The latter were punished for the divisions they had caused in Christ's Body in an especially fitting manner. For their souls (or the corporeal forms which contained them) were cut in half with a serrated iron blade, yielded by gnarled and stocky demons, who were adept at this type of work. Furthermore, each of these razor-toothed blades was heated until it glowed with a ghastly scarlet intensity and horribly flickering luster. And after the soul of each schismatic had been methodically sawed in two, the separated parts would then be crudely joined together again, with molten lead used as a kind of glue to achieve this artificial and imperfect conjunction. Any of the liquified metal which remained after this process was completed was then cruelly poured down the throat of each of the victims.

# The punishments for those guilty of incest, for those who practiced witchcraft, and for those who died in a state of excommunication from the Catholic Church

Next, Frances was led to the locality reserved for the punishment of the souls of those who had been guilty of incest, by forming illicit and impious relationships with persons to whom they were closely connected by blood. All of these souls were held together in one huge vat, which was filled with bodily fluids of the most unspeakable filth and foulness. A band of reptilian demons stood all around this disgusting bath, ready to submerge any soul which attempted to escape from it. Whenever this happened, they would seize the head of the would-be fugitive in their clawed and scaly hands and thrust it deep under the abominable fluid, holding it down without mercy. And all the while, they would sneer and laugh callously.

It should be noted that this place (where those guilty of incest were punished) was not very far distant from the place assigned to the punishment of sexual perverts.[20] After the incestuous souls had been immersed in the vat of filthy fluids for a considerable period of time, other demons would extract them. Then, laying them supine[21] on the ground, they would affix ropes to each of their four limbs. Next, four of the demons there would pull vigorously on each of the ropes, applying all their might to move them in different directions. In due course, and after an indescribably excruciating process of stretching, the body would be ripped asunder, into four parts. But this was by no means the end of the torments for these souls. For the torn quadrants

---

[20] It is to be noted that marriages which were technically incestuous (involving persons who were more closely related by blood than was permitted) were fairly common in the late Middle Ages. Such marriages, which were invalid in the sight of both canon and civil law, were often arranged with a view to keeping wealth and property within a single family line. It seems likely that Frances is including participants in such unions among those guilty of incest.

[21] On their back.

of their body would then be fused back together again, and they would then be returned to the vat of filth.

Following this, Frances, the handmaid of the Lord, was taken to a most shadowy and eerie region, somewhere in the middle of hell. She sensed that this tenebrous[22] and foreboding locale was the place where those who had practiced the forbidden and occult arts of witchcraft were punished. But she was surprised to perceive that it was not only the witches and wizards themselves that were present, but even those who had consulted them or employed their services. Fortune tellers, together with their customers, were there too.

The demons who served in this region were each furnished with a vessel containing an abundance of small globes or pebbles, resembling iron shot. These particles of metal or stone were held over fires (which are everywhere in hell) until they began to glow red. The demons would then seize handfuls of these heated pellets in their thickly-calloused hands and hurl them at the unfortunate souls held there. As may readily be imagined, this procedure caused unimaginable stinging and torment.

There was also a kind of large platform raised up in this area, in the center of which was a huge pit of

---

[22] Dark, shadowy.

unquenchable fire. Various souls would be seized by the demonic servitors there and bound up firmly with ropes or chains, before being thrown headlong into the flames.

At this point, Frances was almost overwhelmed with terror. But her companion angel, Raphael, was quick to comfort her once more. He reminded her that the invincible power of God protected her like an invincible shield, and that what she was witnessing would never, ever happen to *her*, for she was especially beloved by Christ.

Indeed, it was timely that her guardian angel offered Frances these words of encouragement at this point, for what she was about to witness next was even more horrific—namely, the fate of those who had died while in a state of excommunication from the holy Catholic Church.

She perceived that these souls, like all the others condemned to hell, were initially swallowed up by the hideous and monstrous dragon shortly after passing through the grim portals of the netherworld. Yet, unlike all the other souls which were regurgitated after a period of time, the souls of the excommunicated were retained within the body of the dragon. After being swallowed, they entered into his fetid intestines, which were filled with acidic gastric juices and diabolical fecal matter. From there, they descended even lower, into the black depths of the dragon's tail. This tail, as has been noted previously, reached down into the nether-most depths of hell.

Now these deepest parts of the inferno were the hot-test, the temperature reaching such an extremity that even stones liquified and boiled, like super-heated oil or melting ice. Indeed, the agony caused by this heat, which was a thousand times more intense than any earthly fire, surpasses all possible comprehension and imagination!

But this was not all. For to this physical agony was added the constant derision of a chorus of demons, who congregated fiendishly around the tail of the great dragon. They would taunt the souls trapped within the tail ceaselessly, crying out: "O miserable and con-temptible wretches! While you lived, you permitted yourself to be utterly blinded by the lusts and ambi-tions of the deceptive and passing world; and now your sins have bound you up here forever! Now, absconded within the tail of this infernal and diabolical dragon, you shall never again behold the light of day. You did not fear to incur the dire penalty of excommunication and preferred to pursue sin than to retain your precious membership of the Church of God! Now you have all eternity to regret that foolish and evil decision!"

To this, the souls of the excommunicated responded, calling out audibly from within the dragon's tail, in tones of the most heart-rending lamentation:

"Alas for us, who did not cling to Holy Mother Church! Alas for us, who chose sin over communion with Christ's most sacred Body! Truly, there is no one among the children of mortals who can know or understand how intense and overwhelming are our perpetual paroxysms[23] of pain, how appalling and shattering is our shame, and how infinitely and heartbreakingly bitter are the black waves of regret which engulf us!"

---

[23] A sudden attack or spasm.

# The particular torments for those who commit the seven deadly sins

*[Next, Frances was transported to an area of hell where punishments were given for each of the seven deadly sins, which are also known as the seven capital vices. These torments were particularly adapted to the sins or vices to which they pertained.]*[24]

First, she saw the souls which had fallen prey to the vices of pride and ambition. These souls were congregated together in one large chamber. This large

---

[24] This paragraph is an editorial insertion, which serves to make clear the organization of the following series of visions. It is interesting to note that Saint Frances does not enumerate the seven deadly sins (or seven cardinal vices) in the order which is now standard (i.e. pride, greed, lust, envy, gluttony, wrath, and sloth). Rather, she orders them in a way that reflects relationships which she believes exist between the different vices. For example, she places lust after gluttony because she suggests that lust often arises as a consequence of over-indulgence in food and wine.

chamber was subdivided into smaller sections, according to the particular form or expression of pride of which each soul was guilty, since of these there are very many.

For example, those souls which had been infected by an excessive desire for praise or adulation while they lived in the world were tormented by a horde of sharp-tongued demons, who poured out an incessant torrent of acerbic invectives and humiliating mockery upon them. Similarly, there were other torments suited to the various other forms of pride and sinful ambition.

But all the souls who were confined to this region were afflicted by one particular beast, who roamed freely about the whole area. This creature was in the form of a lion but fashioned from burning metal. When it opened its mouth, it revealed rows of razor-sharp teeth. Opening its mouth still wider, it was possible to see a numberless multitude of writhing serpents and venomous toads which dwelled within the beast's throat and stomach. The cruel demons who served in this region would seize the souls condemned to punishment there and toss them into the mouth of the great lion. After receiving bloody wounds from its razor-like teeth, they would pass into the animal's throat and stomach, and there be tormented by the venom of the noisome[25] reptiles and amphibians which abode therein. Finally, they would be expelled through the posterior orifice of the demonic lion, covered with dirt and dung. After suffering this ultimate pain and humiliation, these souls who had once been guilty of pride and arrogance would blaspheme horribly, cursing both their fate and their very existence.

And, all the while, the demons who served in this region would pour out tirades of derision on those souls guilty of pride. They would say: "O, wretched and arrogant souls! While you were in the world, you fought against everyone and everything for your own advancement and glorification. Now you have as your companion and tormentor this most formidable and ferocious feline, this lion of the desert! Be content with *his* company now and for all eternity!"

The angel Raphael then explained to Frances that this lion was, in fact, the soul of Mohammed.[26]

Frances, the handmaid of Christ, then beheld the souls of those who had allowed themselves to be mastered by the vice of wrath. These were all being punished

---

[25] Extremely disagreeable, repulsive.
[26] This language and sentiment about Mohammed expressed here was typical of the time.

with particular torments matching their individual form of anger, irritability, or irascibility.[27] But the common form of suffering which these wrathful souls experienced was that they were all gathered together in the one place, in which there was a monstrous serpent that appeared to be made of living, fiery metal. It had a large and open hood, like that of a cobra, and glared down from above with angry eyes, glowing furiously like burning embers. Its neck was curved forward, so that the hood formed a kind of immense arc. From its hood, there protruded innumerable iron barbs, razor-sharp and blazingly hot. And the demons seized the souls of those who had been guilty of wrath and hurled them towards the head of this angry serpent, so that they collided violently with the piercing barbs in its hood. But once they had landed there, other demons would extract their souls from the chest of the demonic cobra, so that the entire procedure could be repeated again and again. And these tormented souls, now made victims of the vice to which they were prone, did not cease (like all the others) to cry out in blasphemous and resentful agony.

Next, Frances, led on once more by the archangel Raphael, was taken to the place of punishment

---

[27] The quality of being made angry easily.

for those souls which had been infected by greed and avarice. In this place, there was a multitude of vipers with curved, pointed fangs and clawed hands, or talons, extending from their side. These vipers would greedily seize upon each soul with their fangs and clasp the soul firmly with its piercing talons. Meanwhile, it would repeatedly strike them across the mouth and cheeks with its tail, using this in the manner of a whip or scourge. In this place, there was also a huge abyss, which was filled with molten gold and silver. Fittingly, the souls of the avaricious would be plunged into this gleaming but scalding liquid. Meanwhile, the demons who inhabited the region would scoff sarcastically, saying: "O wretched and greedy souls! Your thirst for gold and silver was insatiable while you lived; now you may enjoy having your fill!"

Upon witnessing all of these horrors, Frances, now pallid with terror, began to tremble with fear and astonishment. But her companion, the archangel Raphael, urged her to be strong and to not let her confidence waver. And, having thus encouraged her, they proceeded to the next location which was to be revealed to the saint—the place where those souls which had become infected with the pernicious vice of envy received their just deserts. Here, there was a multitude of writhing, venomous worms. One of these would enter into the mouth of each envious soul and make its way down into the heart. There, it would gnaw away persistently, while pouring forth freely its corrosive and noxious saliva. Meanwhile, a demon standing by would thrust its claw deep into the viscera of the victim, holding firmly the esophagus and the intestine just below the heart, thereby preventing the venomous worm from escaping.[28] After a while, the demons would then tear out the heart itself, still with the dreadful worm of envy writhing within it.

It was the place of torments reserved for those souls who had been guilty of the vice of sloth that Frances was shown next. These slothful souls were all seated on an immense stone square, finished like the top of a gigantic column. They seemed to be uniformly dejected and depressed, with their heads inclined towards the stony floor and their arms hanging limply by their sides. But they were permitted no rest whatsoever, for there were many demons there who ceaselessly pushed and prodded them about, preventing them from ever being able to remain still or sit down, even for a single moment.

---

[28] This vision is to be understood as a spiritual allegory, and Frances was writing according to popular notions of physiology current at the time.

Moreover, there were other demons present who were equipped with sharp swords. They would slash these hapless souls in their sides, causing gaping, open wounds to appear. Then another demon would pour boiling oil into the wounds, saying: "This is for the presumptuous hope you had, making you believe that no effort was required on your part at all to attain salvation!" After this, another demon would thrust a handful of writhing worms into the same wound, saying: "These are for all the vain and empty thoughts that you cultivated, and which festered like worms in your slothful hearts and minds, during your times of lazy leisure and indolent idleness!"

Frances was shocked to see this, but she took comfort and courage from the presence of the archangel Raphael. Before she had fully recovered from the horror of these sights, she was taken to the place where souls infected with the vice of gluttony were punished. The souls, though separated from their original earthly bodies, were given very fat corporeal forms of burdensome weight and egregious flabbiness. A demon there would drag these souls over red-hot coals, and then another would bind them up tightly with ropes, which cut deeply into their flaccid flesh.

From there, these gluttonous souls were cast into a deep pit filled with steaming pitch. Other demons there would then force their mouths open, and pour into these orifices copious quantities of wine, which was heated to boiling, and then they would stuff a multitude of small, noxious serpents into it. While they did this, they would exclaim with sinister glee, "O greedy and gluttonous wretches! You glutted yourself with wine and food while you lived until you grew bloated and obese. Now you can have your fill and more! Enjoy imbibing this boiling wine and consuming these tasty serpents. Yes, these delectable and diabolical delicacies will be your feast now and forevermore!" And upon concluding this taunting mockery, they would erupt in howls of insane, morbid laughter and fiendish, discordant cachinnations.[29]

Close by, there was another place of equally macabre torment. Here were a vast number of souls, bound by ropes to a huge metal globe or sphere. This globe was heated to fiery intensity, so that it glowed with a dull, pulsating redness. Its surface was not smooth, but rather of the jagged and tearing roughness of coarse sandpaper. The souls who were punished there were those who had

---

[29] Raucous laughter.

fallen prey to the vice of lust. Raphael explained to Frances that they were located in close proximity to those souls who were guilty of gluttony, since lust very often arises as a consequence of habitual over-indulgence in food and wine—and therefore may rightfully be considered as the neighbor and kinsman to that vice.

There was a certain hideous demon there that approached these souls which had been bound to the serrated sphere. This demon, whose leering countenance bore an expression of the most vile and indiscriminate lasciviousness, had a tongue of enormous size, which hung from its thick-lipped mouth, almost reaching the ground. This tongue, like the metallic globe, was roughly serrated, and it was covered with viscous and acidic saliva, which glistened horribly. With this huge slobbering tongue, this depraved demon would lick the bodies of the souls who had been guilty of lust, in a lecherous and perversely amorous, but nevertheless heartlessly cruel manner. This disgusting procedure, reflecting the true and bestial nature of lust (which cares naught for the happiness of the other, but only the gratification of the sinful self), was both utterly revolting and indescribably painful!

# The punishments for theft, for dishonoring parents, for breaking vows of chastity, and for selling daughters into prostitution

Next, Saint Frances found herself transported to a grim region of hell where various particular crimes and offenses were appropriately punished. The first of these was the place reserved for thieves of all kinds—ranging from the common bandit or footpad, through to corrupt and fraudulent high officials, nobles, and princes, who misappropriated the moneys entrusted to them.

The souls assigned to this place of punishment were all bound firmly with a black rope, which rendered them completely immobile and robbed them of all freedom and power of movement. And there were three huge, gaping wells or pits in this place, into which the souls of these thieves and robbers would be successively cast. The first well was filled with icy water, so cold that it caused the souls exposed to it to shiver and vomit violently and to assume a ghastly hue of pallid, blood-less blue. The next well was filled with gray, molten lead, which boiled hideously and furiously. Once the souls were extracted from the freezing waters of the first well, their immersion into the molten lead was all the more shocking and stomach-churning, because of the sudden transition. This molten metal caused their skin to blister and crackle, like the skin of a pig that is being roasted, and the tissues beneath the skin begin to cook and emit a disgusting stench.

The third and final well, which followed the pit of molten lead, was filled with repulsive crawling crea-tures of several species—namely vipers, toads, salaman-ders, and scorpions of every kind. Whenever a soul was thrown into this well, the venomous and disgusting creatures would soon begin to crawl into the mouth of the condemned wretch. And because, as mentioned, the souls were bound firmly with hellish, black ropes, each of the damned souls was utterly powerless to defend itself against these unwanted incursions. Then the dis-gusting creatures—serpents, toads, salamanders, and scorpions—would gradually make their way into the viscera of the victim, before finally passing through the body, exiting through the posterior orifice. As this happened, the condemned souls would wail and lament in raucous and demented tones of sheer horror and agony, blaspheming and cursing both themselves and God, in words which were far too impious and appalling to be repeated or recorded in writing.

The next place of suffering which Frances witnessed was where those souls who had dishonored their parents were punished. This included all those who had despised their aging parents or had callously abandoned them to the privations and perils of poverty. Many of these souls, who had mistreated, robbed, or defrauded their own parents, were confined together in one huge vessel, resembling a gigantic flagon. From the interior sides of this vessel protruded innumerable sharp spikes. The flagon was sealed up, so as to prevent any of the souls from escaping; and then tossed about with cruel jocularity by demons. This tossing action caused the souls to come into frequent contact with the spikes, which (of course) wounded them horrifically.

But this was not all they suffered. For within the sealed flagon were also myriads of tiny snakes. These little serpents would leap at (or into) the open wounds caused by the spikes, and then fasten themselves to the flesh with their needle-like fangs, in order to drink greedily of the blood and lymph of their victims.

As for the souls who had insulted or slandered their own parents, these were placed in a different vessel—an ancient and grimy cauldron filled with black, molten tar. And there were various demons standing by this vessel, holding ladles of rusty iron. With these, they would scoop up portions of the boiling opaque fluid and then pour it down the throats of those souls. As they did so, the demons would exclaim: "O wretched ingrates! You disparaged or derided your own mothers or fathers and let foul slander pour forth from your throats. Now, let your throats be filled instead with this burning and caustic tar!"

The next place to which Frances was led was like a dark and shadowy chapel or shrine. But it was filled, not with crosses and sacred images, but rather with ash and smoke, and shards of broken statuary and glass. For this was, indeed, the place of chastisement for those contemptible souls who had committed themselves to religious vows of chastity, but who had covertly violated them. Here there were numberless priests, monks, and nuns, and also not a few bishops and prelates. Molten brimstone trickled down the walls of this chamber like yellow rivulets of liquid fire. Each condemned soul there was wrapped with two pieces of cloth by silent, sable-robed fiends, with a kind of mock-reverence. These garments were then set ablaze, until they burned with searing intensity. And the fiery robe clung closely to the skin of the wretched victims, almost fusing with them in the liquifying heat, while molten brimstone would drip down upon them from the walls.

There were also various other demons hovering about, armed with forks and tridents. With these, they would prod the guilty souls viciously, exclaiming: "You faithless and perfidious souls! You clothed yourselves in the garments of holiness while you lived, and you made a false show of innocence and purity. Yet all the while, you practiced hypocrisy and lust behind closed doors, thereby desecrating your holy vows and insulting Holy Mother Church! Now, most fittingly, you are clothed in the garments of shame and agony, which blaze forth with the flames of perdition—visibly advertising your guilt, so that all may see your true colors, vile and contemptible as they are!"

Saint Frances was utterly appalled by this vision and to witness such a multitude of people who had betrayed their vows of chastity. And her astonishment and shock were augmented by the fact that a number of the souls whom she saw being tormented there were, in fact, religious sisters and priests whom she had known during their lives, and whose goodness and purity she had never once suspected. The archangel, seeing how aghast poor Frances was, held her hand firmly, and said: "O handmaid of the Lord, do not fear! For *you* have always been, and shall always be, absolutely faithful to your one beloved Spouse, Jesus Christ! The fate of these others need be of no concern to you, just as their private lives were not your business while they yet lived." Upon hearing these words of wisdom and comfort from her celestial friend and guardian, Frances once more took courage.

The saint, together with Raphael, then proceeded to the place of retribution for those mercenary and unscrupulous parents who had sold their own daughters into prostitution. These souls, who had been dead to all human decency and oblivious of all the requirements and responsibilities of paternal love, were fittingly placed together in a vast coffin or sarcophagus. Over this coffin were positioned four demons, each in the form of a fierce, snarling dog. These demons in canine form would seize the souls in their ravenous jaws and would savage them furiously with their foul and gore-stained fangs. At times, the grim hellhounds would toss them about, as if in play, from one to the another. And when exhausted with this, one of the dog-like demons would defecate upon the wretched prisoners, before tossing them back casually into the coffin.

There were also other demons there. For the first group described, in the form of dogs, reflected the fact that these parents had engaged in a depravity which was sub-human and bestial. But this next set of demons was concerned with fittingly punishing the greed and avarice which had motivated many of these crimes. Each of these demons was furnished with a huge sack of gold and silver coins, imprinted with the image of Lucifer. With a pair of forceps, it would take one of these infernal coins, and hold it over a fire until it glowed brightly. Then the demon would stamp it firmly upon the chest of each condemned soul, close to the heart. "Alas, you vile sinner, gold and silver were closer to your heart than the innocence of your own daughter! Well, let this coinage—the currency of hell, bearing our Dark Prince's own seal—be imprinted upon that wicked and avaricious heart."

Finally, there was a third set of demons of particularly gruesome appearance. These had jars containing serpents, of a mix of different sizes and varieties. They would seize a handful of these (for the demons of hell are impervious to the venoms of snakes) and deftly bind them with a length of cord. This furiously writhing and coiled mass of snakes they would then affix to the loins[30] of the condemned souls, in a such a manner that they could strike out and bite the area freely. And the demons performing this unspeakable operation would say, with acerbic malice and hatred: "You dishonored the daughter who was the fruit of your own loins! Let these snakes now remind you of your guilt and your incestuous infamy; let the sting of their bites remind you of Divine Justice and human decency, which your own consciences were apparently utterly incapable of doing!"[31]

---

[30] The original text reads *"in illis locis in quibus habuerant gaudium,"* literally meaning, "in those parts in which they took joy." This expression seems to be used as a euphemism for the organs of reproduction, and the translation offered here hopefully conveys the probable intended sense.

[31] The original text, which is rather ambiguous (perhaps deliberately so), suggests that the punishments described here are for those who themselves committed sexual crimes against their daughters. Frances seems to place such offenders in the same category as those who sold their daughters into prostitution.

# The punishments for wicked women, including gossips, foolish virgins, sinful widows, and those excessively concerned with physical beauty

Frances was stupefied by this grim series of visions, but nevertheless she took courage from the reassuring words and presence of Raphael, her angelic companion. Fortified by his supernatural support, she was then transported to the realm where various wicked women were chastised—including those guilty of malicious gossip, foolish virgins, sinful widows, and also those who had been excessively captivated by vanity and concern for the cultivation of physical beauty.

The place where those who were guilty of gossip were detained was replete with a volatile, ever-flickering fire, which filled the air. The tongues of this fire moved about capriciously and maliciously, just like those human tongues which habitually disseminate harmful gossip. To punish those who had become slaves of this heinous and insidious sin (and the related faults of slander and detraction), there was a certain huge demon, dressed in the black uniform of an executioner. This demon had seven heads, each one hideous to behold, and which were all able to move about freely and independently upon the end of a grotesquely distended neck. The first of the heads of this polycephalous[32] and malevolent monstrosity would seize the heart of the guilty souls who were present with its teeth and then forcibly tear it out. Then, the next head would attack the tongue of the gossiping soul and bite at it ravenously with its own sharply pointed teeth, eventually ripping it from the mouth completely. It would then toss the severed tongue to the third head, who would place the bloody organ into a blazing furnace, until it began to cook and crackle. The fourth head would then extract it from the fire and insert it forcefully and violently back into the mouth of the unfortunate soul.

The fifth head would attack the soul's eyes viciously, until the eyeballs ruptured and the ocular juices spilled

---

[32] Many-headed.

out. The next demonic head was equipped with a long, pointed tongue that would dart sharply into the ear of the soul, drawing out through these same orifices, pulsating, gray lumps of brain tissue. The seventh and final head of this demon would snap at the nose of the victim, scratching and wounding it until it bled profusely.

Other demons were also present there, whose role it was to pour out continuous insults upon the souls who had indulged in the vice of gossip and detraction. "O contemptible and vile wretches!" they exclaimed. "You once used your eyes and ears to pick up nasty information about your neighbors. You constantly poked your noses into that which did not concern you. You used your heart to nourish malice and malevolence. And you used your puny, pusillanimous[33] brains to invent lies, and your tongues to spread them. And now you suffer all that is due to you!"

Next, Frances beheld the place where foolish and hypocritical virgins were punished. These were women who had professed vows of chastity and who had preserved their physical virginity, and who made a great show of pretended sanctity and external piety. But inside their hearts, they had harbored thoughts

---

[33] Small-souled.

and feelings that were quite contrary to their public vows. For they had either nourished spite and malice towards their neighbors, or cultivated the evil root of pride, or sought eagerly after sensual luxuries and the adulation of others. These souls were bound with iron chains; and fiery robes, resembling the habits of religious sisters, were placed upon them. And a demon inhabiting this area would taunt them constantly, saying: "You foolish virgins, you made such a proud display of outward purity: but inside, you were filled with impurity and vice! The robe of apparent innocence which you so hypocritically wore in the world is now exchanged for a robe of scalding fire—for such a garment is indeed more befitting to your true character!" And, having concluded this mocking discourse, the demon would then erupt in an ear-jarring cacophony of wicked laughter.

Not far from this place was the area where sinful widows received the retribution due for their offenses. These were all bound by ropes to one tree of prodigious size—a gnarled, knotted, and most sinister oak. Depending upon the nature of their sins, some were tied around the neck, while others had ropes affixed to their feet or arms.

This eldritch[34] and ghoulish tree bore a great multitude of large acorns. These appeared, at first glance, to be fine, wholesome nuts, aglow with fullness and vitality. But a second and closer look revealed that they were, in fact, filled with writhing maggots; and that putrid, black juices oozed out of them. These maggots would drop from the nuts upon which they fed into the mouths of the souls of the wicked widows suspended from this tree. There was also a dragon that circled the tree and would frequently strike out with its talons or jaws to inflict pain upon these wicked souls. This dragon could speak, and in a reptilian, sibilant[35] voice, it would say: "O wretched souls, who were not content with the state of holy widowhood! Instead of pursuing prayer and good works as behooved you, you threw yourselves wholeheartedly into gossip, gambling, drunkenness, idleness, gluttony, vanity, and lust. Such indeed were the foul things you sought in life. Now let these foul worms and maggots fill your desires! You bound your souls to the evil tree of the sinful and wicked world by means of the multitude of your vices. Now you are bound to this tree of filth and shame, forever and ever!"

---

[34] Weird and sinister.
[35] Hissing or snake-like.

Finally, Frances was taken to another place of torment—where those women who had been excessively concerned with the cultivation of physical beauty were duly punished. This included all those females who had used spells, charms, and philters[36] to increase their ability to captivate men, and those who had used cosmetic artifices to enhance their looks in a deceptive manner. Frances was aghast to note that some of them had living serpents coming from their heads, in place of hair. The angel Raphael explained to the saint that these were all the souls of women who had been obsessed with the beautification of their hair while they lived, at the expense of proper attention to their domestic and religious duties. There were others who were robed in what appeared to be fine and brilliant dresses, but these were fashioned not from silk or soft fabric, but from closely woven strands of flickering fire. And in the places where gemstones are customarily worn (such as the neck and fingers), glowing coals were positioned instead.

And there were demons who exclaimed derisively to the first group (that is, those with snakes in place of their hair): "While you lived, your hair was your greatest concern and pride. Now let these living serpents decorate

---

[36] A potion to arouse sexual passion

your scalp!" Meanwhile, other fiends addressed themselves to the second group, who were dressed in the garments of fire. "During your time on earth," they said, "you wished desperately to appear bright and radiant before others. Well, hopefully these vestments of flame will fulfill your wish! And your vain hearts yearned for glowing gemstones, for rubies of sparkling red, and diamonds of scintillating clarity. Well, let the glow of these red-hot coals and the glimmer of their luminous sparks satisfy your shallow desires! And, finally, you sought to have all men pay you their undivided attention. Well, instead of the attention of mere mortal men, you now have countless undying demons, who will never cease to pay you court, even for a single moment!"

# The particular torments reserved for sinful preachers, hypocritical and mercenary confessors, and corrupt prelates

To her great relief, Frances was transported from the gruesome place of punishment reserved for wicked women. But the next region she visited was no less dreadful. For it was the area where iniquitous clergy received their fitting retribution. Led on by her celestial companion, Raphael, Frances bravely entered this place of abject confusion and chaotic darkness, reverently invoking the grace and protection of God.

The first group whom she saw being punished were sinful and duplicitous preachers. This group included all those who had failed in their duty to correct the wrongdoings of others, motivated either by fear or by hopes of gaining favor or reward. There were also present among them all those preachers who had mixed human falsehoods with the divine Word of Truth, and thus led their hearers into error or even unwitting heresy. The souls of such sinful and negligent preachers were sent into a furnace filled with opaque, contorted, and swirling shadows of almost palpable density. In addition to this suffocating and oppressive obscurity, there were a multitude of hideous adders and vipers, which struck out relentlessly with envenomed fangs and darting, forked tongues.

There were also demons there in the form of huge, black hounds. These wolf-like, phantasmagoric[37] creatures would squat down and, in a canine manner, emit foul-smelling, viscous dung into the mouths of those preachers who had lacked the courage to correct the faults of others, as their duty had demanded. "Since these preachers had been so reluctant to say anything which may have caused offense while they lived," explained the archangel Raphael to Frances, "they are now making up for it, by being compelled to swallow this disgusting dung in copious quantities!"

There were other demons present in that region, too, carrying vats filled with molten brimstone and

---

[37] Ghostly or sinister.

pitch, and they held in their hands large spoons or ladles. With these, they would take a scoop of the boiling liquid and pour it down the throats of certain souls. "These are the ones who mixed falsehood in with the Truth!" said Raphael to Frances. "They let the toxic filth of heresy come out of their mouths in their preaching, and so now their mouths are being stopped up with this super-heated and sticky brew!"

In another place close by, Frances then saw the souls of mercenary and hypocritical confessors who had failed to administer the sacrament of penance with honesty, justice, and integrity. These souls were placed in a gigantic set of scales, which swayed about unsteadily and vertiginously,[38] as if at random. Beneath these scales, a blazing fire burned intensely, its flickering, crimson flames reaching up to the condemned souls to scorch and sear them. And there were grinning demons standing by, too, who shouted out words of condemnation and derision, saying: "You miserable and iniquitous wretches! You were once elevated to a position of sacramental authority by the Holy Mother Church, yet you abused your position. For you failed to weigh people's sins in the scales of justice and truth, but acted

---

[38] Suffering from vertigo or dizziness.

according to self-interest, cowardice, and caprice. Now *you* yourselves are placed in these faulty scales, to do all the penances which you failed to impose on others!"

Finally, she saw a vast chamber where the souls of corrupt prelates[39] were punished. Frances observed that this group included bishops, abbots, cardinals, and even (to her great shock and horror!) certain popes.[40] The torments imposed upon these souls took a particular and distinctive form. Firstly, a large helmet made from red-hot metal, and molded into the shape of a bishop's miter, was cruelly forced upon their heads. Secondly, they were bound firmly onto a chair in the form of an episcopal throne. This chair was then raised up by ropes and turned upside down, leaving the souls uneasily and awkwardly suspended therefrom, with their heads towards the ground. Finally, a great wolf

---

[39] The term prelate is most commonly used as a synonym for bishop, but can also include other high-ranking ecclesiastical leaders, such as abbots and superiors of religious orders.

[40] The observation of certain popes in hell is found also in Dante's *Divine Comedy*. Very prudently, Saint Frances (unlike Dante) does not identify any particular Roman pontiffs as having deserved eternal condemnation. In the era when Saint Frances lived, there were also numerous antipopes in existence, including eight during the span of her own life. These antipopes made illicit claims to the papacy, often supported by violent military action. Her vision here may well refer to such antipopes.

that was covered with coarse gray bristles, and had salivating jaws and eyes like burning embers, prowled about beneath them restlessly. It would direct vicious and voracious bites at their suspended souls and snarl in a chilling and bestial manner. There was also another demon standing by, saying: "You iniquitous prelates, who were entrusted with high offices in the holy Church of God! You were supposed to protect and lead the flock of Christ, yet you were not true shepherds at all, but rather ravenous wolves disguised in sheep's clothing. Well then, this wolf of hell is surely fitting company for you now!"

By this stage, Frances was almost overcome by terror and exhaustion at all she had witnessed. But the angel Raphael once more urged her to take courage, reminding her that what she was witnessing was only a vision, and that she was not really physically present there at all. Upon hearing this, the saint felt her heart strengthened, and her courage and fortitude were once again restored.

# The names and activities of the principal demons of hell

After the ghoulish and sinister visions described in the preceding chapters, Saint Frances next related to her spiritual director certain other things which had been revealed to her. Among these secret revelations, she had come to understand the mystery of why some of the angels had fallen from grace and rebelled against the love and majesty of their omnipotent Creator. She also learned the details of their names and their respective roles in the hierarchy of hell.

Of those angels who had fallen from heaven, a third of them abide in hell (Frances said), a third inhabit the air, and a third inhabit this world and tempt human beings. But those angelic spirits who allied themselves to Lucifer in his ill-fated rebellion are, like him, strictly confined to the regions of hell. And they shall never be released from there, except by divine permission, when this world shall fall into ruins on account of human sins, at the end of the age. These rebel angels (who became the demons who abide permanently in hell) are the worst and most evil of all. Those who inhabit the air and those who live in the world are those who took neither the part of God nor of Lucifer in the attempted primordial rebellion, but who tried to remain as neutral onlookers.

Frances related that in hell, there are three great demonic princes who are bound together with their leader, Lucifer (or Satan), and who had been his chief allies in his attempt to seize power in heaven. Each of these had once been a glorious angel of exalted rank but were now the most evil and malignant (as well as the most powerful) of all the demonic horde. Lucifer himself has primary place as supreme ruler and monarch of hell. But the first of his allies or generals is called Asmodeus. This Asmodeus had formerly been one of the cherubim, but now presides over all the vices and sinful lusts of the flesh. Next was a demon called Mammon, who had formerly been from the angelic choir of the Thrones; but now is leader of the vice of avarice and all the sins which spring therefrom. The third in rank of the henchmen of Satan was a demon called Beelzebub. Before his fall, he had been a member of the angelic choir of the Dominions; but now he presides over all forms of idolatry and superstition, and in particular the crimes of witchcraft and sorcery. He is ruler and potentate over the pernicious darkness and vain phantasms which cloud the minds of those mortals who immerse themselves in occult and forbidden practices.

These three principal demons, or dukes of hell—Asmodeus, Mammon, and Beelzebub—never leave the infernal domain of Lucifer himself, but always remain within the Tartarean[41] realms of hell. But they are able to send forth other malign demons, who are their vassals. These diabolical thanes[42] whom they send forth as emissaries normally also dwell in the nether regions of the abyss, but sometimes can venture forth (with the permission of God) into the world to perform some malicious action or to instigate some disaster or catastrophe in the human, or natural, world. These demons, when they enter our world, either remain in the air or sometimes even walk among human beings to carry out whatever their evil mission happens to be. But they do this only with the permission of God and according to the inscrutable decrees of Divine Providence.

---

[41] An adjective derived from *Tartarus,* a classical name for hell or the underworld.

[42] Vassals or servants.

As described earlier, hell is divided into three different levels—a lowest, a middle, and an uppermost region. These different levels were each inhabited by fallen angels, according to the rank which they had formerly occupied in the celestial hierarchy before their ancient fall. Those fallen angels which had come from the highest three choirs (the Seraphim, the Cherubim, and the Thrones) are consigned to the very lowest and darkest of the levels of hell. Here, they both experience torments of the most unimaginable and severe intensity and are also responsible for inflicting befitting punishments upon the very worst of sinners. This set of demons, who were formerly the most glorious and exalted of all the angels, are subject to the direct dominion of the arch-fiend himself, Lucifer, who is the lord of lies and the prince of darkness.

For this fallen angel, known as the Bearer of Light and the Morning Star,[43] is both the supreme patron and the ultimate victim of pride. He rebelled against God, not to attain to any real pleasure, happiness, or rest but rather for the sake of nothing more than pride, that is, for the vapid glorification of his own sense of self. This vice is surely more futile and pernicious than

---

[43] The name *Lucifer* means bearer of light and was also a title traditionally given to the morning star.

any other, for it does not even gratify the senses (as some other sins do), but is merely an empty shadow, like imaginary gold or counterfeit currency. For status and glory, which are the principal objectives of the vice of pride, bring no real happiness, but merely toil, anxiety, and unrest. Thus, pride is both the most harmful, and the most pointless, of all sins.

The next level of hell, which is the middle region, is occupied by those demons who, before the fall, belonged to the angelic choirs of Dominations, Powers, and Virtues.[44] These fallen angels are tormented there, and they are responsible for inflicting suffering on the souls who have been consigned to that region for punishment. Their leader is the demon Asmodeus, a fallen Cherub. This Asmodeus is prince and patron of all sins pertaining to the desires of the flesh, for his own heart is a veritable cesspit of insatiable lust. It was this same fiend who was smitten with infatuation for Sarah, in the book of Tobit, and maliciously killed the seven men who attempted to marry her.[45]

---

[44] In the original text, there seems to be an error in ordering of the angelic choirs, with the location of the Principalities and Virtues being reversed from the conventional sequence. Since this is presumably a simple scribal or authorial mistake, the translator has restored here the usual ordering.

[45] See Tobit 6:13.

In the uppermost level of hell are the rebel angels who came from the three lowest ranks, namely the Principalities, Archangels, and Angels. This uppermost level of hell is the *least* horrible of the three— but needless to say, even its terrors and torments far exceed all human words and mortal imaginings. The leader of these demons had fallen from the celestial choir of Thrones and is named Mammon. He is the prince of the vices of avarice and greed, and he is the patron of all the sins and crimes springing therefrom. Indeed, Christ Himself identified him as such, when He declared: "You cannot serve both God and Mammon."[46] The impossibility of serving both Mammon and God arises from the idolatrous nature of avarice,[47] for it makes a counterfeit deity of earthly gold and silver. Alas, how many people are led into fatuous[48] and futile devotion to these passing, deceptive, and ephemeral things, which promise so much, yet can confer neither life nor happiness on those who pursue them!

The demons who are under the command of Mammon—that is, the fallen Principalities, Archangels, and Angels—are the most numerous and exhibit an

---

[46] Matthew 6:24.

[47] See Colossians 3:5.

[48] Foolish.

incredible diversity of forms and appearances. These very frequently go out into the world in order to tempt human beings. And thus it is that the vice of avarice and greed expresses itself in a bewildering multitude of different sins and crimes, including theft, deception, corruption, exploitation of others, neglect of domestic and religious duties, and miserliness. Hence it was that the apostle Saint Paul sagaciously described avarice as "the root of all evil."[49]

The third demon who has been noted as one of the principal companions and henchmen of Lucifer was Beelzebub. This shadowy, mysterious, and utterly repulsive entity was once a member of the noble and glorious angelic choir of the Dominions. This was before his alliance with Lucifer in his wicked rebellion against the Supreme Divinity had caused him to be cast down to the kingdom of pain and misery, the land of chaos and eternal night. This Beelzebub was assigned the grim role of master of the shadows and darkness, which are virtually omnipresent in hell. This hellish and nebulous darkness is of a different nature from common, earthly darkness, which is merely an absence of perceptible light. For the darkness of hell

---

[49]  1 Timothy 6:10.

is oppressive and suffocating, like a kind of viscous tar or pitch. It not only obscures the capacity of vision to perceive clearly, but obliterates clarity, form, and sense itself; like a kind of palpable cloud of confusion, despair, and meaninglessness.

Beelzebub is also the patron and prince of all forms of witchcraft and sorcery. For these nefarious practices cast dark shadows and confusion over human minds and draw them away from the radiant and liberating splendor of the eternal truth. The extent of these crimes, though hidden, is very great and widespread indeed— almost beyond what can be believed or even imagined!

Various demons, who are under the command of either Lucifer, Asmodeus, Mammon, or Beelzebub, are constantly sent forth into the world, to tempt human beings. The wicked spirits sent forth by Lucifer (that is, those who were formerly Seraphim, Cherubim, or Thrones) inhabit the air, and they generate tempests, hail, and thunderstorms. They also implant the malignant and noxious seeds of pride into human hearts. The thanes[50] of Asmodeus are active in stirring up the lustful desires and the sinful impulses of the flesh. Those sent forth by Mammon prey upon souls who are already

---

[50] Servants or vassals.

weakened by the vices of pride and lust, and they cause these souls to be filled with avarice and greed for worldly lucre. Finally, the demonic ministers sent out by Beelzebub seek out carefully and cunningly those who have been frustrated in the fulfilment of the impulses of pride, lust, and avarice. Once they have found such unfortunate and miserable souls (and there are a great many of them!), they turn their thoughts and inclinations towards the dark arts of sorcery, witchcraft, and the occult; or, in some cases, cloud their minds utterly with the poison of heresy.

Frances revealed to her spiritual father that when one of the demons sent forth to tempt a particular person was not successful in its wicked endeavor, it would be struck with the utmost confusion and despair. Sometimes, it would then proceed to try to tempt another individual or try to bring about some harmful or wicked effect in another way. With the permission of God, demons could also enter into the bodies of brute animals, causing madness, viciousness, or illness in these hapless victims. Other times (again, with the permission of almighty God), they would take control of the bodies of living human beings. Such demonic possessions are occasionally made manifest in horrible and grotesque displays, but more often than not they are completely unsuspected by others. Demons could also impersonate ghosts, claiming falsely to be the returned spirits of the deceased.

Whenever a demon did succeed in tempting a soul into the paths of sin, it would remain on the earth after the soul it had conquered had been taken off to hell. Following this, the demon would then move on to another soul and begin to tempt it. With each successive victory, the demon would become ever more cunning, more subtle, more wicked, and stronger. Frances also revealed that any given demon does not try to tempt more than one soul at a time but focuses all its attention and power on overcoming the resistance of just one individual.

# The power of the holy name of Jesus

Saint Frances next declared that she observed that whenever the most holy name of Jesus was pronounced with true devotion, all of the demons (including those in hell, those in the air, and those in this world) are constrained to genuflect.[51] They do this not out of their own free will and desire, but as if compelled by some superior and unseen force.

The saint then testified how once she had uttered the name of Jesus during a conversation with her spiritual father, and she had witnessed a multitude of demonic entities who were then present (but invisible to everyone else) genuflect and touch their heads to the ground in unwilling and resentful reverence. She also declared that the greater the devotion and the more perfect the love with which the holy name of the

---

[51] See Philippians 2:10.

Savior was pronounced, the more torment and pain the demons then experienced.

When sinners utter the name of Jesus in vain or blasphemously, she said, the demons are still compelled to genuflect. But in these instances, the torment which they feel is mixed with a degree of perverse joy, because the sin of taking the Lord's name in vain has been committed. The holy angels in heaven likewise all genuflect whenever the name of Jesus is pronounced. When it is uttered in vain or blasphemously, they do so without joy, but still with infinite reverence. But when the name of Our Lord is spoken with true reverence and love, the joy which the celestial multitude experience is so great and intense that it can scarcely be described or imagined.

A similar effect was observed when other divine names and titles were spoken, and likewise that of the most glorious Virgin Mary. The utterance of any of these names causes waves of joy and jubilation to flood the heavenly homeland, and it causes all the blessed entities who reside there, both human and angelic, to exult gloriously. But the degree of effect the pronouncement of such names has is proportionate to the sanctity and merit of the person who says them.

Frances related how she could see her own guardian angel (who was almost always visible to her) respond whenever she spoke the name of Jesus, or when anyone else spoke that most holy name in her presence. It would smile radiantly, with the purest and highest joy, and then genuflect with the utmost reverence and delight. The sight of this filled Frances with an unspeakable happiness and made her heart burn with the most ardent and ecstatic love of the Savior and His holy name.

# The condition of the
# souls in purgatory

In the name of the most Holy Trinity, here begins our discourse on purgatory, in which, with God's gracious help, the visions which were shown to blessed Frances and which she revealed to her spiritual father will be described.

After the conclusion of all her various visions of hell, which are described in the chapters above, the saint related that she was then led away to see purgatory. This realm, she testifies, consists of three divisions or levels—lower, middle, and upper. She perceived at the entrance to purgatory a great sign made of shimmering crystal. It bore the following inscription, written in lettering of vibrant, opalescent brilliance:

"BEHOLD, THE REALM OF TRUE PURGATION,
A LAND OF HOPE, NOT DESOLATION!

OH, MANY PAINS ARE HERE, FOR SURE—
BUT THEY WILL NOT FOR LONG ENDURE!
FOR WHEN ITS TIME DECREED HERE
    ENDS,
EACH  SOUL  FROM  HENCE  GOD'S
    MERCY SENDS
TO  HEAVEN'S  KINGDOM  OF  PURE
    LIGHT,
TO  REIGN  IN  HOLY  LOVE'S
    DELIGHT!"

As Frances entered purgatory, she sensed once more the invisible presence of her celestial guardian, the archangel Raphael. This mighty angel said to her: "This realm is called purgatory, for the souls who are here are in the process of being purged of their sins and guilt. For this reason, it may also be justly called The Place of Hope! The lowest of the three regions of purgatory is filled with flames, like hell. But the flames here are of a different quality and nature to those in hell. For the fires of the inferno are black and lightless, whereas the flames of purgatory glow with a vivid red and give forth radiant light. The light of these purifying and cleansing fires illuminates the souls which are here with divine grace. Through this illumination, they come to realize the saving and liberating truth, and to understand that their term of purgation is fixed and finite."

Frances saw the location of the souls in purgatory was proportionate to the gravity of the sins which remained on their conscience at the time of their death. For those who were guilty of more grave and serious sins, they were immersed in the lower levels, where the fire was more intense. It was also revealed to Frances that for each and every unatoned mortal sin a soul had committed, they would be obliged to do a period of seven years of penance.[52]

Frances next turned her gaze to the demons who are assigned to service in purgatory. Every soul has its own demon assigned to it, who stands at its left side. This demon constantly reminds the soul of its guilt and the gravity of the offenses it had committed against the Almighty, saying: "Lo, these pains you suffer very rightly on account of the crimes you have perpetrated

---

[52] It should be noted that this is not an official teaching of the Catholic Church as stated. She is referring to the temporal punishment of a grave sin, of which St. John Chrysostom states, "it is not enough that sin has been pardoned; the wound which it has left must also be healed by penance." See *The Catechism of Council of Trent*, p. 301, CCC 1472. However, although the Church teaches the necessity of temporal punishment of grave sins, it does not specify the period of time involved.

against your God, who created you and redeemed you with infinite love and generosity! Instead of following the truth, you preferred to be seduced by the illusions and deception of demons, like me—who are all fiends and liars. How often you succumbed to temptation, ignoring the gentle voice of the Lord, to listen instead to the nefarious whisperings of the world, the flesh, and devil! So now, you are paying the price of your iniquity and doing just penance for your countless sins." These reproaches, together with the hideous aspect of the vexatious companion demon who uttered them—not to mention the cleansing fire which abounds in purgatory—were a source of very grave suffering for the souls who were serving time there.

Frances noted, however, that apart from these verbal reproaches and their annoying presence, the demons in purgatory did not torture the souls to whom they were assigned in any way. For the sufferings in purgatory, though undeniably severe and painful to endure, are not inflicted as punishments. Rather, they are the workings of celestial mercy and necessary to fulfill the requirements of Divine Justice. Their intent is not to harm but rather to heal. As such, these sufferings resemble surgical operations which are painful or medicines which are difficult to consume; they are admittedly deeply unpleasant and irksome, but at the same time wholesome and healthful.

The saint also perceived that the souls in purgatory cry out continually. But this crying out is of a very different nature to the hopeless vociferations of the souls who are damned to hell. For in hell, the wailing and moaning of the souls is the sound of utter despair and agonized desolation. But in purgatory, the crying out was rather an expression of sincere and heart-rending penitence, and it was even of gratitude at the mercy of God. While these cries were far from exultant or joyful, they nevertheless were infused with a kind of firm hope and spiritual beauty, and they were nothing like the black and jarring cacophony of despair which resounded ceaselessly in the fiend-haunted netherworld of the inferno.

This firm hope and strength, which could be detected in the tones of the cries of penitence that came forth from the denizens of purgatory, sprung from the fact that each of these souls realized that all that it currently suffered was merely temporary and a necessary part of its preparation for heaven. Indeed, these souls, though they endured pains and torments of varying degrees of intensity, all knew with absolute certainty that, in due course, they would arrive at the ineffable joys and radiant splendors of the kingdom of God.

As mentioned earlier, the demon who was assigned to each soul in purgatory to remind it constantly of its sins and the ways in which it had offended its loving Creator, was situated at the left of each soul. Frances next went on to say that, at the *right* side of each soul, there stood an angel—an entity of indescribable beauty and magnificence and bathed in the splendid glow of ethereal refulgence. This angel was, in fact, the very same spiritual entity who had been appointed by God to serve as the guardian angel of the soul during its earthly life, and who now continued to protect and comfort it in purgatory. Frances observed that the angel would encourage the soul it accompanied by communicating to it all the prayers and alms which were offered for its sake by relatives and friends who were still alive.

This guardian angel, who stood at the right of each soul, would also respond to the vexatious demon, who stood at the left. Whenever this demon would remind the soul of the sins and vices of which it had been guilty during its mortal life, the angel would respond by reminding the soul of the deeds of charity and piety which it had performed. It would also remind the soul of the good works it had intended to do, but never actually put into practice; and also, of the times when it had sincerely and earnestly fought against some temptation, whether successfully or unsuccessfully. For God, the most just of all judges, considers not only actual words and actions, but even the unseen desires of the heart and the hidden intentions of the soul. This merciful Lord never demands of us more than His grace gives us the strength to do and never tests us with any temptation of trial which is beyond our capacity to endure.

# The glories of heaven

The attention of Frances was then drawn to the souls which were taken from purgatory and brought to the Kingdom of Heaven. These were ones who had completed their assigned term of penance, purgation, and purification, and so, they had ascended to the very uppermost and lightest portion of the realm. The sight of a soul departing from purgatory was truly amazing and caused Frances's heart to be filled with unbounded joy and wonder.

The glorious Queen of Heaven would descend on a cloud of golden light. She was robed in a garment of azure blue which glimmered like a sapphire, and upon her head, she wore her twelve-starred crown of celestial majesty. Her beauty was such that Frances could find no words to describe it, but which simultaneously far exceeded both the radiance of the noontide sun in all its splendor and the serenity of the moon as it floats through a tranquil sky.

The Mother of God, having descended to purgatory, would then lead the fortunate soul that had completed its time of purgation from there into heaven and take it to the choir of angels among which it had merited to be placed.[53] As Blessed Mary, together with the soul, passed through the various angelic choirs, there would be immense joy and jubilation breaking out at the sight of another one of the beloved children of God being taken to its blessed and everlasting homeland. But the greatest rejoicing took place in the choir to which the soul was assigned as its destination. In that celestial choir, there would be a great festivity of exaltation and holy mirth.[54]

As for Frances, she was given the grace to be able to witness the departure of many souls from purgatory and their ascent to heaven in the company of the Mother of God. When she revealed or described this to her spiritual father (which she frequently did under holy obedience), her face would begin to glow, as if set aflame with celestial fire. This came about particularly when she called to mind the ineffable sweetness of

---

[53] This should not be interpreted as implying the soul actually becomes an angel once it arrives in heaven, but rather that it will be placed in the company of the angels in heaven.

[54] Gladness accompanied by laughter.

the singing of the angels, together with the chorus of the souls of the blessed. For the pure and mellifluous harmonies of this eternal hymn of praise exceeded all that the human mind could grasp or imagine. When Frances recollected this and attempted to describe it, it was as if her soul would melt with ecstatic joy, like a piece of soft wax liquifying in the warming presence of some heavenly fire.

She related that the souls of the blessed in heaven were of greater perfection and nobility than the angels. But the song of the angels remained more beautiful and purer, and the melodies which they sang were more subtle, agile, and sweet. Nevertheless, the song of the Queen of Heaven entirely transcended that of both the angelic multitude and all the souls of the saints.

But Frances confessed that there were many things in her visions of heaven which she could not comprehend, and that those things which she did witness, she perceived only in an unclear and obscure way. This was, she said, because she remained in the state of sinful mortal life and did not yet possess the complete purity which was requisite to behold these things perfectly.

The Beatific Vision itself, which is the experience of gazing upon the highest mystery and glory of the divine Trinity, was received in varying ways in the different choirs of angels and different ranks of the saints. For those who were higher and exalted enjoyed this wonderful vision with greater clarity and completeness, according to their rank and station. And the souls of those saints who had been more distinguished in merits and virtue during their earthly lives possessed more capacious and subtle powers of perception and comprehension in heaven and could therefore enjoy the Beatific Vision there more fully and gloriously.

———◦◦◇◦◦———

Here concludes the visions of Saint Frances of Rome of hell, purgatory, and heaven. These she communicated faithfully to her spiritual director, who diligently recorded them in writing. In sharing all of these visions, Frances, the handmaid of Christ, subjected herself with the utmost humility to the teachings, judgement, and magisterium of Holy Mother Church—for she desired nothing more dearly than both to live and to die in perfect communion with this one, holy, Catholic Church. Amen.

# SELECTED OTHER VISIONS OF SAINT FRANCES OF ROME

*as recorded by her spiritual director,*
Canon Giovanni Matteotti

# The visions of Saint Frances commence

A mong the various graces which the Lord conferred upon his handmaid Blessed Frances in this present life, there are a great many which you, O reader, will discover in the lives of very few other saints. For she was granted an angel, who (as she herself testified) was from the second chorus of the celestial court, that is, one of the holy Archangels.[55] This archangel assigned to her as a companion and servant was quite different from the guardian angel which is granted to every soul. For this archangel was constantly present to her, appearing in visible form, in the guise of a human figure—namely, a boy of about nine years old, clad in a tunic as white as snow. And the face of this heavenly being was more radiant than

---

[55] It is not entirely clear whether this angel (or the second angel, from the choir of Powers) is to be identified with the archangel Raphael, who accompanied Frances on her visions of hell, purgatory, and heaven.

the sun and so brilliant that Frances was not normally able to look directly upon his glowing countenance.

But there were two occasions on which Saint Frances *was* able to look directly upon the face of this holy archangel. Once was when her spiritual father was speaking to her about this holy being. At that time, she was able to see clearly and distinctly the eyes, hair, and features of her celestial servant. The other occasion was when Frances was being attacked viciously by a multitude of evil spirits. At that time, Frances cast her eyes towards her archangel, feeling that she was about to be completely overcome by the demons which vexed her. And the angel stood before her, with a face of such radiance and hair of such glowing brilliance that the evil spirits were utterly overwhelmed and put to flight by his mere presence. Indeed, such was the brightness of the archangel who was the constant companion of Saint Frances that she never had the need of lamplight or candlelight to perform any task, either in the day or at night.[56]

During the first year of her widowhood,[57] Frances had renounced and abandoned all earthly concerns and

---

[56] This angel who constantly went before Saint Frances and lighted the way is linked to her veneration as the patron saint of automobile drivers.

[57] 1436.

business in order to devote herself entirely to the interior life. Shortly after this, on the 21st of March 1436 (the feast of Saint Benedict), when she was giving thanks to God for the blessings and graces she had received from Him, she sensed that another angel had been assigned to her. This time, the angel was from the fourth choir of the celestial court—that is, one of the Powers. She at once felt that she was receiving a more abundant outflowing of grace from the Most High, insofar as this second angel was of such an exalted rank. Thereafter, whenever Frances was being assailed by some evil spirit, this second angel would put it to flight immediately, not by any display of radiance or brilliance (as the first angel had done), but rather with an invisible spiritual strength and invincible mystical power.

It happened that once when this handmaid of Christ, Frances, was saying the seven canonical hours for her beloved and divine Spouse, she beheld this second angel in a physical form. Above its head rose a column of light of miraculous splendor, which seemed to reach up to the very heavens. She saw also that it held in its hand three branches of gold, similar to the branches of a palm tree. The angel was using these branches to spin golden thread, fashioning three separate plaits[58] of differing thickness, each of the most glorious brilliance. These it continued to spin without cessation in her sight until the feast of the Assumption of the Blessed Virgin Mary,[59] in the year 1439. It then explained that it had fashioned three bands, one consisting of a hundred threads, another sixty, and another thirty. By this, it signified the various states of Christian life—contemplative, apostolic, and lay—returning respectively a hundred-fold, sixty-fold and thirty-fold harvests, according to the words of the Gospel.[60]

Frances's mind was elevated above all worldly concerns and very often exulted into ecstatic contemplation of celestial realities. This happened whenever she received the Body of Christ in the most holy Sacrament of the altar, but on many other occasions also. During these periods of transcendent contemplation, it was as if her soul entered into a mystical inner chamber, and she became totally oblivious to the outside world.

But when any of her servants or other members of her household noticed this happening, it was as if Frances would have preferred to undergo martyrdom than for her special graces to become known to others. For she desired

---

[58] A pleat or braid of material.
[59] August 15.
[60] See Matthew 13:8.

earnestly for her experiences of mystical union with God to remain a cherished secret between her and her Beloved, to be shared with God alone and no mortal being.

———⊷◇◇◇◇◇⊶———

Once it happened that when Frances was absorbed in prayer and holy meditations, suddenly she saw a group of twenty-six demons before her! These were of horrible and grotesque appearance, and they hurled insults at her while brandishing burning firebrands viciously. And they said: "This is the wrath of God which shall be visited upon the city of Rome, on account of its countless sins and iniquities! Yes, two of our number have been appointed as executioners, to go forth and destroy the Eternal City!"

Upon hearing this, Frances was filled with deep anxiety and anguish, both because of the horror of the vision itself and because of the devastation which threatened to fall upon the people of Rome. So, she prayed fervently, committing herself entirely to the will of God. But one of the demons, wishing to confuse Frances, assumed the form of the Savior and hovered in the air before her. But the saint could not be deceived and recognized this apparition as a mere trick.

However, at that point, a *real* vision appeared. The glorious Mother of God stood before her, wearing a crown on her head and holding the infant Jesus lovingly in her arms. On one side of the Blessed Virgin was Saint John the Baptist, and on the other side stood the apostles, Peter and Paul. These three saints were all kneeling before holy Mary, praying earnestly that she should save the city of Rome from destruction.

Then Frances heard Our Lady speak in a voice of indescribable sweetness and transcendent majesty: "Great is the mercy of the Lord! Because of the intercession of these three saints, the sentence of death passed against Rome has been revoked. But unless the Roman people depart from their wickedness, a worse fate shall eventually befall them!"

Now, shortly after Frances had seen this vision, a most remarkable sign occurred. For lightning from heaven struck in three different locations in Rome. One of the lightning strikes happened at the belltower of the Basilica of Saint Peter, another was in the belltower of the Basilica of Saint Paul, and the third was in the Lateran Basilica of Saint John the Baptist. This happened in the year of Our Lord 1430, in the month of July.

# A vision following the reception of the Blessed Sacrament[61]

On a certain day, when Frances had received the most holy Body of Christ in the Chapel of the Angels, in the Church of Saint Mary in Trastevere,[62] for almost half an hour she remained enraptured in heavenly contemplation. When she returned to herself from this ecstasy, her spiritual director asked her to relate to him all that she had experienced. Since he made this request with the authority of holy obedience, with the utmost humility Frances told him what she had seen.

After she had received the Blessed Sacrament, she was (she said) taken in spirit to a vast and beautiful meadow that was filled with the most delightful grasses and flowers. In the middle of this meadow stood a fountain, fashioned from gleaming alabaster, from

___

[61] Frances experienced this vision in April of the year 1431.
[62] A suburb of Rome.

which came forth water of sparkling clarity. The water issuing from the fountain flowed throughout the field in crystalline streams, and everywhere it passed, blossoms of indescribable beauty sprang up.

Seven human forms approached the alabaster fountain and drank deeply of its waters. Frances was also then filled with an eagerness to drink from it. This she did, and at once experienced a consolation and delight which exceeded all possible description. Then she saw upon the fountain certain inscribed letters of in radiant gold:

> "The Lord of love, through tender grace,
> Shall draw to His divine embrace
> Each soul that burns with love for Him
> And purifies itself from sin."

After reading these verses, Frances (while still in a state of rapture) then prayed: "I implore you, my sweetest Lord and my perfect love, conform my will completely to Your own. Liberate me from all my anxieties, for I stand before You worried and forlorn. . . ."

# A second vision following the reception of the Blessed Sacrament[63]

On another occasion, when Frances had received the most holy Body and Blood of the Lord, following the advice of her spiritual director, she was engaged in intense prayer, again in the Chapel of the Angels, in the Church of Saint Mary in Trastevere. She was then taken up into ecstasy and remained perfectly immobile for about half an hour, completely insensible to the outside world. Later on, her spiritual director inquired of her what she had experienced during the time of that mystical trance.

Under holy obedience, Frances replied that she had been drawn up in her spirit and positioned in an enormous and most magnificent temple, unlike

---

[63] This occurred on the Solemnity of the Holy Trinity, in the year 1431.

any earthly edifice. There she had perceived a person who glowed with the utmost radiance, descending for the heights of heaven. This mysterious, celestial entity spoke to her and said: "Behold, I am the burning Tabernacle of God!" Then, despite the fact that there was no apparent opening through which she passed, Frances herself was then taken inside this visionary Tabernacle!

Inside the holy Tabernacle, she heard music of a sweetness beyond all imagining and smelt a fragrance of indescribable delight. She also noticed there a kind of large basin, or bath, of gleaming white marble. Within this bath was a kind of clear, sparkling fluid, which glittered with the color of purified gold. Within this golden liquid, there floated marvelous pearls, gemstones, and other nameless but wonderful treasures of ineffable beauty.

The spirit of Frances was then seized with an irresistible longing to grasp some of these treasures for herself, but she found that she was utterly unable to raise her hands to do so. So instead, acting upon an overwhelming spiritual impulse, she brought her head to the bath, and she was able to drink a single drop of the mystical and celestial liquid. And (as she related to her spiritual director) this single drop of divine, ambrosial[64] refreshment was sufficient to fill her entire soul with the most perfect delight and sustenance.

---

[64] Resembling *ambrosia,* or a kind of heavenly nectar.

# A third vision following the reception of the Blessed Sacrament[65]

On another occasion, when Frances, the handmaid of Christ, had received the most holy Body of Christ, she was praying (as was her custom) in the Chapel of the Angels, in the Church of Saint Mary in Trastevere. Once again, her spirit was absorbed into a mystical rapture, while her body remained immobile in a trance-like state for a considerable period of time.

When later questioned by her spiritual director, Frances related that, in her spirit, she had been transported to a vast plain or field wonderfully illuminated with brilliant light. This field was of incredible beauty, its grass glowing with the rich verdure of a precious emerald. And in that field was a wondrous

---

[65] Frances experienced this vision in August of 1431.

Lamb, whose fleece shone with a radiance exceeding that of the purest snow. Standing close by this Lamb (which was very manifestly none other than the divine Lamb of God) was a noble youth of great delicacy and beauty. He wore upon his shoulders a garment resembling a dalmatic, and a crown woven from flowers and a laurel rested upon his head. Surrounding the divine Lamb was also a chorus of other figures in human form, wearing beautiful vestments of a variety of colors and crowned with roses. These human figures (whom Frances recognized to be the souls of the saints) were paying devout homage to the Lamb and exulting jubilantly in its presence. The aforementioned youth, wearing the dalmatic, appeared to be leading all the others. As they passed before the Lamb, they would sing:

> "Let us all the Lamb adore
> With joyful hearts, forevermore;
> Let us to His glory sing,
> For He alone is King of Kings!
> His love He promised to impart
> To each and every humble heart:
> This love is our supreme reward,
> And this pure Lamb, our only Lord!"

Frances perceived also that there were several streams or rivulets which flowed through this field of astonishing beauty. Each of these streams—which were five in number—was of a different color. The noble youth who was vested in a dalmatic led Frances, together with the chorus of the saints, to each of these rivulets in turn.

The first of them flowed with waters of rich red, which glowed with the roseate luster of a precious ruby. And the angelic youth here exclaimed, "Behold, this first ruby-hued rivulet represents the ardent and invincible love with which Christ redeemed the human race. For it was in the crimson stream of blood that flowed from His wounded side that salvation poured forth for the world!"

The next stream was filled with a liquid of a milky white color, which shone like polished ivory or newly fallen snow. And the youth here said, "This second stream, of immaculate purity and untainted clarity, represents holy innocence. For it is innocence and purity of conscience alone which may ascend the holy mountain of God, to behold there the supreme goodness of the Creator!"

The third stream flowed with waters of shimmering, verdant green. "These are the waters of hope," exclaimed the youth, "for hope is the virtue which imparts vitality and fertility to all the good and perfect things for which love strives!"

The fourth stream was filled with waters of bright azure blue, resembling the color of the vault of heaven on a cloudless, sunlit day. The youth said, "This stream represents the virtue of holy obedience, which leads the soul on the gentle ways of righteousness, and which brings it finally to blessed and blissful union with the divine will."

The fifth stream was crystal clear and perfectly transparent without any hint of coloring at all, like a precious diamond without fault or flaw. "These transparent and clear waters are the stream of purified faith, unpolluted by any taint or cloud of doubt and fear, and as strong and inviolable as a faultless diamond. The soul that drinks of these waters of perfect faith and which immerses itself in their crystalline purity shall never be separated from the highest beatitude of divine glory!"

At this point, as Frances related, her vision came to an abrupt end, and she found herself once more in her mortal body, in the chapel in which she had been praying. She was then filled with bitter anxiety, desolation, and sorrow that her most glorious vision had been terminated so suddenly. "Alas," cried the saint sadly, "I have been cruelly deceived! For in my heart, I firmly believed that I would remain in the place of splendor and beauty forever, but now I have returned to this earthly valley of tears and the drab dreariness of mortal life. Yet I know that God never deceives anyone. . . ."

At this point, a certain evil spirit suddenly became visible to Frances. She then realized that it had been this malign entity which had implanted in her mind these dangerous feelings of anxiety and bitterness. So, calling upon the grace and mercy of God, she was able to dispel this wicked demon, together with the emotions he had generated. And, having done so, she gave thanks and praise to her loving Lord for revealing to her in this vision a most wonderful foretaste of the beauty and splendor of the celestial kingdom which awaited her in the future.

# Frances has a vision of a ferocious dragon, which represents an attempted rebellion against the papacy[66]

Once when Saint Frances was engaged in prayer and meditation in her bedchamber, she was taken up into an ecstasy. A little later, when she returned to her normal senses, she found herself overcome with a feverish feeling of intense heat and so opened a window. Looking out of the window into the night sky, she admired the vault of heaven and the multitude of shining stars which shone down upon her. As she did so, she lovingly contemplated the power and glory of the divine Creator of such wonder and beauty.

But then suddenly, a violent storm broke out, and she saw a most terrifying black dragon appear in the sky.

---

[66] This vision occurred in July of 1432.

Its ferocious jaws were open, and a blazing and fetid fire poured forth in acrid torrents from its mouth. It flew through the air with the utmost rapidity, and wherever it went, tempestuous gales and lightning followed.

Frances was terrified by this vision. So, she called upon her guardian archangel-companion, who comforted her and assured her of his unwavering protection. The saint noticed also that a great multitude of souls, both male and female, were following the wicked dragon through the sky. Then an evil spirit or devil, which seemed to be Satan himself, appeared before her and spoke in a horrendous voice. It said: "This crowd, whom you see following the dragon, are all those who obey my commands and desires!"

It was later revealed to Frances that the dragon which she beheld in this terrible vision represented a certain ambitious and seditious military commander, who was then leading a rebellion against the authority of the pope. This same military commander would go on to sow great civil agitation and cause much damage to the Church and the people of Rome.[67]

---

[67] The editors of the *Acta Sanctorum* identify the rebellious military officer represented by the dragon in this vision as Niccolò Fortebraccio (1374–1425). He was a notorious *condottiero,* or leader of a mercenary army, and he attempted to seize control of Rome by force of arms in the early 1430s.

# Frances receives a bouquet of roses from Saint John, the apostle and evangelist[68]

Once while Saint Frances, the handmaid of Christ, stood in her bedchamber in prayer (as was her usual custom), she was taken up into a mystical ecstasy. Now at this time it happened to be the feast of the apostle and evangelist Saint John,[69] and in her vision, she witnessed this solemnity being celebrated in heaven.

Saint John the apostle himself stood there, and he gave Frances a bouquet of twenty roses of peerless and transcendent beauty. Of these roses, five were brilliant white, five were rich red, five were a splendid blending of red and white, and five were of a deep violet hue. He

---

[68] This vision occurred on the feast of Saint John the Evangelist, in December of 1434.

[69] December 27.

then said to her, "Give to your archangel-companion[70] these flowers, for he knows how to handle them most fittingly!" This Frances did, and her archangel carefully placed them in a lovely vase of transparent crystal. Once they had been placed in this vase, the roses released a perfume of unbelievable and overwhelming sweetness, surpassing that of any earthly fragrance.

Then Saint John said to her, "O Frances, the five white roses you see are for your purity of heart, while the five red roses are for the burning love of Christ which consumes you so ardently. And the five roses which combine the colors of red and white reveal the perfect and indivisible union of your own will with that of God.

"You will notice also that the roses which are in the lower positions have their petals closed, while those which are higher up are fully opened. This signifies that the human heart ought to close itself to the things of this lower world and open itself fully only to the glories of heaven—just as you do!

"Finally, the five roses of a deep violet hue signify the virtue of faithful and profound humility. Out of the other virtues—purity of heart, burning love, and faithful humility—the most glorious and excellent

---

[70] Presumably, this angel is Raphael, who is identified elsewhere as Frances's particular guardian.

fruit of holy obedience springs forth. Truly, this holy obedience is a most sweet and enchanting fragrance in the presence of the Lord; just like the celestial perfume of these mystical and holy roses which I have bestowed upon you, beloved Frances, as a special reward for your singular merits and sanctity!"